INFLUENTIAL
L!VES

HE LI
OTO

CHRIS ROCK

COMEDIAN AND ACTOR

Philip Wolny

Enslow Publishing
101 W. 23rd Street
Suite 240
New York, NY 10011
USA
enslow.com

Published in 2019 by Enslow Publishing, LLC.
101 W. 23rd Street, Suite 240, New York, NY 10011

Library of Congress Cataloging-in-Publication Data

Names: Wolny, Philip, author.
Title: Chris Rock : comedian and actor / Philip Wolny.
Description: New York : Enslow Publishing, 2019. | Series: Influential lives
| Includes bibliographical references and index. | Audience: Grades 7-12.
Identifiers: LCCN 2018010813| ISBN 9781978503441 (library bound) | ISBN
9781978505193 (pbk.)
Subjects: LCSH: Rock, Chris—Juvenile literature. | Comedians—United States—
Biography—Juvenile literature. | African American comedians—Biography—
Juvenile literature. | Actors—United States—Biography—Juvenile literature. |
African American actors—Biography—Juvenile literature.
Classification: LCC PN2287.R717 W65 2018 | DDC 792.702/8092 [B] —dc23
LC record available at https://lccn.loc.gov/2018010813

Printed in the United States of America

To Our Readers: We have done our best to make sure all websites in this book were active and appropriate when we went to press. However, the author and the publisher have no control over and assume no liability for the material available on those websites or on any websites they may link to. Any comments or suggestions can be sent by e-mail to customerservice@enslow.com.

Photo Credits: Cover, p. 1 Jason LaVeris/WireImage/Getty Images; p. 4 Rick Kern/WireImage/Getty Images; p. 9 Dimitrios Kambouris/WireImage/Getty Images; p. 11 Bob Gomel/The LIFE Picture Collection/Getty Images; pp. 14, 17 Michael Ochs Archives/Getty Images; p. 22 © HBO/courtesy: Everett Collection; p. 25 Dorling Kindersley ltd/Alamy Stock Photo; p. 27 © Paramount/courtesy Everett Collection; p. 32 Ted Thai/The LIFE Picture Collection/Getty Images; pp. 36, 108 © AP Images; p. 39 Jeff Kravitz/FilmMagic, Inc/Getty Images; p. 43 Moviestore collection Ltd/Alamy Stock Photo; p. 45 © 20th Century Fox/Everett Collection; pp. 48, 68, 81 AF archive/Alamy Stock Photo; p. 50 Fotos International/Archive Photos/Getty Images; p. 54 Everett Collection; p. 57 New York Daily News Archive/Getty Images; p. 62 Kevin Winter/Getty Images; p. 64 RGR Collection/Alamy Stock Photo; p. 66 CBS Photo Archive/Getty Images; p. 73 Jemal Countess/Getty Images; p. 76 Peter Kramer/Getty Images; p. 78 James Devaney/WireImage/Getty Images; p. 85 Ron Galella Collection/Getty Images; p. 89 Bruce Glikas/FilmMagic/Getty Images; p. 93 Jon Kopaloff/FilmMagic/Getty Images; p. 94 AFP/Getty Images; p. 98 KMazur/WireImage/Getty Images; p. 101 James Devaney/GC Images/Getty Images; p. 103 Paul J. Richards/AFP/Getty Images; back cover and interior pages background graphic zffoto/Shutterstock.com.

Contents

Introduction 5

Chapter One
A Rock Grows in Brooklyn 8

Chapter Two
A Rising Star. 21

Chapter Three
Live, from New York—It's Chris Rock! 34

Chapter Four
Bringing the *Pain*. 46

Chapter Five
At the Top of His Game 60

Chapter Six
A Cut Above the Rest. 72

Chapter Seven
Up Close and Personal 84

Chapter Eight
"If It Ain't New, It's Through!" 96

Chronology 111

Chapter Notes 114

Glossary 122

Further Reading. 124

Index 126

Chris Rock has built a stand-up comedy legacy and is revered by audiences, critics, and other comedians.

Introduction

. . . .

Oне Saturday evening in November 2016, the audience of NBC's weekly live comedy sketch show, *Saturday Night Live*, got an extra treat. Comedians Dave Chappelle and Chris Rock had popped in that week as special guests. It was the week following the election of Donald Trump to the US presidency, and many Americans were still shocked by the outcome.

In the sketch, Rock and Chappelle played two black election-night party guests in a room full of their panic-stricken white friends as they watched the results come in. The sketch was a commentary on how many white liberals were unprepared for a Trump win, while African Americans were completely unsurprised. For Rock, participating in the sketch was a homecoming to a show that had helped put the comedian on the map early on in his career.

It was also a reminder of how the talented comedian, writer, actor, and director—a veteran of television and film—had branched out in a career spanning more than three decades but had kept a sensibility that still made him one of the most popular and critically acclaimed comedic talents of his generation. Rock had begun his career with bit film roles but received his first recognition on the national stage with *SNL*.

From humble beginnings as a working-class youth in Brooklyn to tough years proving himself on the stand-up comedy scene after dropping out of high school, Chris Rock has defined edgy and smart stand-up comedy for several generations of comedy fans. His aggressive and animated onstage presence, along with famous bits that have attained iconic status among fans, make Rock both a fan favorite and what the industry sometimes calls a "comedian's comedian." His uproarious and thought-provoking takes on race, marriage, parenting, relationships, and dozens of other topics have sometimes inspired as much outrage as laughs. Still, they remain an irreplaceable aspect of his art and comedy brand.

Additionally, Rock has appeared in dozens of films, in both minor and major roles. He has also been a writer on many projects, a few of which he also starred in and directed, and even one documentary about the cultural phenomena surrounding African American hair. Rock has also made a name for himself as a sought-after master of ceremonies for award shows and other events, including high-profile annual ceremonies like the MTV Video Music Awards, two appearances hosting the Academy Awards, and much more.

Rock's output has been prolific and influential. Few comedians working today have worked as hard on their craft or inspired as many young comics as Rock. It is time to take a look at the influential life of the hilarious Chris Rock, both in his public persona as a funnyman and keen observer and in the personal journeys that he has taken as a father, entertainer, and human being.

CHAPTER ONE

A Rock Grows in Brooklyn

· · · · · · · · · · · · · · · · · ·

It was 1965 in Andrews, South Carolina, just outside Myrtle Beach. On February 7 of that year, Julius Rock and his wife, Rosalie, or Rose, welcomed their first of seven children into the world. Christopher Julius Rock, though born in the South, would soon relocate with his parents up north. The Rocks were part of a much larger trend called the Great Migration. Starting around 1914 through the 1960s, millions of African Americans and their families left the South to seek their fortunes, mainly in factories in the upper Midwest, in New England, and on the West Coast.

When he was just a toddler, Chris and his family moved to the Bedford-Stuyvesant neighborhood in Brooklyn, New York—often referred to simply as "Bed-Stuy." At the time, in the 1960s, New York was beginning to experience budget troubles. Crime and other social ills hit New York City and other urban centers from the late 1960s through the 1990s.

By the time Chris lived there, Bedford-Stuyvesant's population was mostly black. While crime and gang problems were common, many of the African Americans who lived there owned their own homes. In addition, the area was known as a center of black culture, food, and commerce in New York, as famous in its own way as Harlem in upper Manhattan. Like many predominantly black areas of the city, it had its problems. However, it could also be a quiet place where children played, neighborhood elders held forth on their stoops, and people absorbed the energy and sense of community daily.

Chris Rock was raised in a big family that included (*left to right*) brother Brian, mother Rose, and brother Jordan. The Rocks valued hard work and strict discipline.

On Decatur Street

Much of the neighborhood was full of well-built brownstones. The Rocks lived in one, located at 619 Decatur Street. Some of the neighbors even called their bit of Brooklyn "Decatur Towers," a joking but affectionate nickname for their beloved block.

The patriarch of the family was Julius Rock. His son later described the elder Rock, who usually worked as a union delivery truck driver for the *New York Daily News*, as funny and engaging, but also hardworking, reliable, and responsible. His dad also drove a cab sometimes, once the family got bigger. On certain nights, when he had finished his delivery route, he would enlist his eldest son to help him sell off extra bundles of the *Daily News*. His work ethic was transmitted to Chris and the other children, who all were required to get a job once they turned fourteen. For Chris, that meant working at McDonald's and a chain discount store called Odd Lots. With a very large family to support, care for, and guide, father Julius was quite literally one of the two rocks that kept the household stable.

The other was Rose Rock. Chris's mother was an educator and ran a preschool and day care center. She was a nurturing but no-nonsense mother and later described her parenting style in this way: "I'm the boss. I'm not your friend."[1] She was referring both to the many children who had come in and out of her classrooms, as well as her family.

At home, the Rocks were a loving family, but not one without rules. Discipline and setting limits were part of the Rocks' parenting philosophy. Besides helping the

This aerial view shows a section of the Bedford-Stuyvesant neighborhood of Brooklyn, New York, pictured here in 1968. Known as Bed-Stuy for short, the area has been a capital of African American culture for decades.

kids build character, it was necessary to keep a large family running smoothly. It was also helpful because money was frequently tight. Julius and Rose owned their own home but had to make ends meet in various ways. Sometimes this meant cutting down on or skipping little luxuries or counting on the end of the month, when they collected rent from tenants to whom they sublet one of their floors.

There were also the foster children Rose and Julius took in over the years. As many as seventeen passed through their household. Some became as close to Chris and his brothers and sister as flesh-and-blood siblings. Though they could be serious, Rock says both his parents had a sense of humor, and he credits them equally in his own development as a young class clown and the family's go-to funny person.

A Rough and Tumble Youth

The Rock children would need every bit of guidance. While they had a loving family, the temptations of 1970s New York City street life were many. From petty crime, to robbery, to the drug trade, it was tougher to stay away from trouble in Bed-Stuy than other places. By the time Rock was a teenager, according to the *New York Times*, violent crime in his area was 80 percent higher than the average for New York and the murder rate was twice the already-high city average.

In an interview with Mo Rocca for CBS News, Rock credited his dad with helping him and his siblings stick to the straight and narrow. He acknowledged how lucky he was to grow up with both parents in the house and to have limits and boundaries as a child. Some of the kids he knew growing up came from broken homes or had parents who worked too hard to be around much.

"Where I'm from," he said, "it was simple things like, 'Hey, don't hang out on the corner.' . . . I remember being on the corner a couple of times, and the next thing I know, I'm in a police line-up. All I need is some woman sitting there with a black guy, and if she points at me, I'm going to jail, and I hadn't done anything."[2] He added, "If you were into rough stuff, it was rougher. But if you're like me and had the two parents and rules and regulations in your house, it wasn't as tough."[3]

As the oldest, Chris was charged with many responsibilities, including minding some of his younger siblings. He took care of things like helping prepare breakfast in the morning and getting some of the kids ready for bath time. Chris also had some perspective on all that his father did for them, due to his age and position in the family.

> "I love what's happened to me, but when I was a kid, I wanted to be the president of the United States."[4]

The Original Kid of Comedy

Even as a child, from as young as age five, Chris began to crack up family members, relatives, and friends. He could even dissect television comedy—mostly situation comedies, or sitcoms, and figure out when a punchline was coming after a setup. Chris built an early critical and

Comedian and actor Flip Wilson's popular and groundbreaking 1970s variety show had a big influence on Chris Rock.

Chris Rock's Influences

The 1960s and 1970s were a time when new, fresh voices—black and white—were pioneering new forms of comedy beyond the simple punchline jokes of earlier eras. The zany antics of Steve Martin, tales of frustration and anxiety from Woody Allen, and Lenny Bruce's boldness and storytelling all had an impact on the budding young comic. Bill Cosby's and Richard Pryor's stand-up albums, including their long observations on human nature and behavior, inspired Rock greatly. So did Flip Wilson, one of the first African American comedians to enjoy major success on television. Yet another was comedian and activist Dick Gregory, who combined cutting wit and an unapologetically black comedy persona that he developed in the underground black comedy and music clubs— sometimes dubbed the "chitlin circuit"—and spread to mainstream and white audiences, with great success.

analytical streak when it came to comedy. He told the *Guardian* in 2008, "Even as a young kid, I knew *Brady Bunch* wasn't funny. By the time I was eight, I could tell you what was about to happen in a sitcom. I could see all the jokes coming."[5]

He always devoured comedy wherever he could find it, some of it parent-approved, the rest the result of sneaking around late at night. With his parents, Chris would catch Flip Wilson's variety show on television. After dark, he savored the slightly more adult comedic takes of Bill Cosby, Richard Pryor, and George Carlin, among others. He sometimes tried to sneak a peek at whoever was doing stand-up on *The Tonight Show*, hosted by Johnny Carson. While he liked comedians of all kinds, it was only natural that he would sometimes gravitate to the unique perspectives of black comedians in particular.

Buses, Bullies, and Breaking Out

Rock's parents were convinced that sending him to their rougher area schools would be a bad idea. Their bright son needed a better education and could avoid bad neighborhood influences. He has joked that while the average suburban child might cover a neighbor's house in toilet paper as a Halloween prank, his neighborhood was different. "The guys in my neighborhood were going to rob a store."[6]

Soon, Chris was getting bused across the borough of Brooklyn to schools that were mostly or entirely white. Tensions between whites and blacks in New York easily boiled over then, even more so than nowadays. It was

This picture was taken around the time Rock was first launching his comedy career. The once bullied teen had already made it to heights of stardom that his classmates could scarcely imagine.

often teenagers and children who saw the most fallout from these divisions. In every grade after he started bussing, Chris was usually the only black boy in his grade, and often the only one in the school itself, though there were usually two or three black girls, too.

Of being bused and experiencing often-shocking racism in early 1970s' Brooklyn, Chris told James Lipton on *Inside the Actors Studio*, "It's the defining moment of my life. One on hand, it made me everything I am. On the other hand, it really screwed me up badly. I was bused to school into a poor white neighborhood."[7] Part of the problem, he said, was racism, but the other was that boys in particular were cruel and acted out physically. He had also been small and skinny for most of his childhood and suspects that he probably would have gotten hazed or picked on regardless of his skin color.

Reverend Rock

One non-comedian who influenced Chris was his grandfather, the Reverend Allen Rock, a preacher. Rock told James Lipton on *Inside the Actors Studio* that his grandfather was among the funniest people he had ever known. Seeing his grandfather preparing sermons and practicing them later influenced his own comedy writing and brainstorming. "A lot of my comedic style is probably from my grandfather, watching him write the sermons. He never really wrote the sermon, he would just write the bullet points. To this day, I don't really write jokes, I just write the bullet points, and then I go."[8]

The racial dimension just made things more intense, of course. Besides getting assaulted daily, he heard racial slurs often many times a day. "I was made to feel really bad every single day," he related to *Ebony* magazine. "My spirit was broken every day. Lucky for me, I had a lot of love at home."[9] He would be mostly quiet and keep a low profile in school, but when he got home, the real Chris would come out to shine.

Eventually, the constant level of bullying he continued to receive in high school was so traumatic and depressing that it drove him to quit school entirely. "It just zapped my wanting to be in a classroom, and I dropped out. I had no personality in school, because I was abused," he revealed to *Best Life* magazine.[10] Sadly, all he could look forward to in school on a daily basis were regular beatings and the constant use of the "n-word" directed at him. Chris had never been an honors student, but the bright young man could hardly summon up much enthusiasm for doing very well in the abusive environment he found himself in.

Nevertheless, he credits this bullying with helping him build character. He acknowledges how lucky he was because his home life provided enough of a foundation that bullying did not drive him to harm himself, give up on his dreams, or commit suicide, like many kids who are bullied and see no way out. Later, Rock even thanked his bullies for giving him strength. He now feels that every time he was punched, spit on, or kicked down the stairs, he says—usually by the same group of boys—it helped strengthen him. The comedian admitted, "On one hand, I would have had a much more normal childhood and been happier at that time if I had gone to a black school. But if I wasn't bused to the white school, I would probably have a normal job now. I wouldn't be a comedian. In a weird way, those people made me who I am." [11]

Coming of Age

Rock had no concrete plans when he became a high school dropout at age seventeen. He would earn his General Educational Development (GED) diploma instead. As a teenager, he worked at the Red Lobster seafood franchise, toiling as a busboy. He also got a job as an orderly at a psychiatric hospital. He even leveraged his father's connections at the *Daily News* to score a job unloading trucks. A thin and slight man his whole life, he got a workout filling random orders that came in through a night shift when he had to load 50-pound (22.6-kilogram) newspaper bundles. Some of his most cherished memories were being able to see his dad occasionally on the job and the funny stories of the older characters that worked shifts alongside him.

Rock later admitted that the truck-loading job was miles ahead of his experience at Red Lobster, where he worked emptying customer plates and loading up the dishwasher. Still, the sharp, intelligent young man working at menial jobs was just beginning his journey. Rock would soon take the plunge that would launch him from family cutup to comedy legend.

CHAPTER TWO

A Rising Star

. . . .

Y ears before, when he was either seven or eight, Chris Rock had noticed the names scrolling in the credits of a sitcom. He imagined then that he would put his natural talent to use one day and perhaps even write for television himself. Now that he was his own man, he switched his focus somewhat from his childhood dream and decided to do stand-up instead.

The First Stand-Up

There are differing accounts among family members and other associates about when Rock decided to take the real plunge and do his first set in front of an audience. Some believe it was a dare from somebody in the neighborhood, part of an ever-changing audience of neighbors and passers-by that would trade quips with Rock and his brothers on their front stoop some evenings.

However, Rock remembers it somewhat differently. In 1983, Rock was just eighteen years old. Perhaps his

Eddie Murphy's 1983 smash comedy concert film *Delirious* had a formative impact on Rock's own comedy and ambitions.

biggest hero at the time was Eddie Murphy, the stand-up sensation and *Saturday Night Live* alumnus who had gone on to become a big Hollywood star. That year, Murphy had broadcast his comedy special, *Eddie Murphy Delirious!*, also released as a live comedy album, and it had floored Rock. One night, he was on line to get tickets to see Murphy perform at Radio City Music Hall and was flipping through the pages of a newspaper to kill time. He noticed the listings for comedy sets and open mic sessions at some comedy clubs nearby. As Rock told the *Guardian* later, "I don't know what it was, but something in my head said walk away, so I did."[1]

He took the walk to Catch a Rising Star, a comedy club on Manhattan's Upper East Side. It was audition night, and he stood on line again to get a lottery ticket that might give him an opportunity to get onstage. Soon, Rock realized that his ticket (a lucky number seven) had just won him the chance to do stand-up for five minutes. Energized, he quickly put together some material on paper while waiting for his slot. On stage the rookie got some big laughs. In the jargon of the industry, he had "killed it."

The club offered him work whenever he wanted it. It was a great opportunity for a new talent. According to an interview and feature in *Rolling Stone* magazine, he came back about half a dozen more times and killed it each time. Then, he says, he bombed, and continued to bomb for the next three or four years. It was a harsh but common lesson in how merciless and cruel show business could be. It also underscored just how intensive a career in stand-up comedy could be. Many comedians work for years before they achieve even minor success, much less comedy specials on cable television networks or offers for their own sitcoms. Nevertheless, Rock continued to press on.

Paying Dues

With sets at Catch a Rising Star, Rock would expand to other venues. He remembers those years of having something to prove and distinctly recalls being the energetic but inexperienced skinny kid with bad teeth and a Jheri curl hairstyle, a "wet" look that was popular at the time. Meanwhile, he still had to work to make ends meet.

He even spent a year attending Brooklyn's Kingsborough Community College, earning credits in the school's broadcast journalism program. Around this time, he would go to classes, head to his job for a shift, and then end up in Manhattan late at night, trying his routines out onstage. This grueling late-night schedule, when he would finish up at 2 or 3 a.m., would sometimes take a toll on him. Some nights, Rock would even sleep in his car near school or in front of work to save time getting there.

A Big Break

It was 1986, and Rock was performing at the Comic Strip Live, on Manhattan's Upper East Side, the oldest comedy showcase club in the industry. Comedy legends like George Carlin, Richard Pryor, Robin Williams, and many others had taken the stage there. One of the club's alumni and Rock's hero, Eddie Murphy, was in the audience that night.

The Comic Strip comedy club was instrumental in Rock's early career and in the careers of many other established comics. Even today, Rock performs secret sets at comedy clubs to test out new material.

In his appearance on *Inside the Actors Studio*, Rock related how he had a deal with Lucien Hold, manager of Comic Strip Live, to stack chairs for the club in exchange for a late-night performing slot. While he was stacking, the novice comedian was stunned when Eddie Murphy came out of the bathroom. While Murphy remains respected nowadays for his legacy, at the time the movie star was at the top of the world. For Rock, it was like seeing the president of the United States.

Hold introduced Rock to Murphy, who asked the manager what time Rock was going on. Rock responded that he wasn't going on that night. Murphy responded by telling Hold to put Rock up next. While Rock did his routine, the crowd laughed, and cutting through the loud din of the club, he heard Murphy's distinctive laugh. He knew that whatever happened from then on, he had arrived, at least in his own mind. Even better, Murphy told him that he was impressed with his chops. He asked Rock to fly out to Los Angeles the next day to work on something with him.

> "I got to hang around the real Eddie Murphy. Not Dr. Doolittle. Leather suits every day Eddie. Elvis."[2]

That night, bursting with excitement, Rock went home to pack and prepare. While his mother was skeptical and a little bit suspicious of her son cavorting with the flamboyant and (in her mind) hard-partying celebrity, a brief meeting between Rock, his father, and

Murphy the following day was held, and Rock was soon on a plane to Hollywood.

Rising Higher

Rock had never had a real role in a film before. He usually doesn't count a nonspeaking extra role in a hip-hop musical drama from 1985, *Krush Groove*, in which he appeared momentarily during a fight scene at a club. Now he was going to be paid $600 for a speaking role in

A still from the 1992 film *Boomerang* features Chris Rock and his idol and mentor Eddie Murphy in a scene together. Rock played a wisecracking employee at Murphy's character's advertising company.

an Eddie Murphy film, *Beverly Hills Cop 2* (released in 1987). He played a parking lot attendant that Murphy's police character interacts with at Hollywood's Playboy Mansion. That trip to Los Angeles marked Rock's first time flying in an airplane and also the first time he had ever stayed at a hotel.

While staying in California, Rock took advantage of Murphy's connections and appeared in his first HBO broadcast, *Uptown Comedy Express*. The announcer in the special's advertisement described Rock as an "Eddie Murphy protégé." Actor, comedian, and future talk show host Arsenio Hall even joined Rock for a couple of sketches that were included in the special.

Now that he had his foot in the door, he pushed it open farther. He began to get roles in comedy and action dramas. One of the first was as a records clerk with the Miami Metro-Dade Police on the popular NBC police drama *Miami Vice*. Rock was amused and starstruck by his time on the television show's set because funk and soul legend James Brown appeared in a cameo role during the episode entitled "Missing Hours," which aired November 13, 1987.

It was an appearance in a black action comedy, however, that would set the tone for the kind of projects that Rock would achieve success in throughout the late 1980s and early 1990s. Many of his projects were associated with the growing hip-hop culture that now encompassed not just music, but film, comedy, and other disciplines. The film *I'm Gonna Git You Sucka* was written and directed by Keenen Ivory Wayans, a rising star himself who, along with his siblings, would create and star in *In Living Color*, a weekly sketch comedy show with a predominantly black cast. The movie was a tribute to and satire of the outlandish, street-smart, and often tongue-in-cheek blaxploitation films of the 1970s. Rock proved to be a scene stealer as the patron of the fast-food joint who asks for "just one rib." The scene became an iconic one and was often quoted by comedy fans, long before the era of movie quotes and scenes going viral online.

Amid Success, a Personal Tragedy

Suddenly everything seemed to be going Chris Rock's way. His career had jump-started, and things would only

One of Comedy's "Dirtiest Dozen"

In 1988, a cable television variety show on the USA Network, *Night Flight*, featured a clip of Rock during his tenure at Catch a Rising Star. The producer of the show, Stuart Shapiro, was putting together a comedy special featuring hot up-and-comers. The special would end up featuring a six-minute bit by Rock. In it, he made risqué jokes about the stereotypical character Aunt Jemima (featured on the pancake brand of the same name), commented on the stereotyping of black teens, talked about his Bed-Stuy upbringing, and mused on the racism surrounding the 1988 presidential candidacy of activist leader Jesse Jackson. The special was called *Comedy's Dirtiest Dozen* and also featured the likes of Tim Allen, Jackie "the Joke Man" Martling, and the late Bill Hicks.

go higher in the coming years. But in November, Rock and the rest of his big family would suffer a crushing blow. The father and husband they had loved so much had been suffering from diabetes and a peptic ulcer condition. He ended up in the hospital from complications arising from his ulcer rupturing. After a failed operation to help him, Julius Rock died.

Like all of his siblings, Rock was crushed. He revealed to *Ebony* in 1997, "It was by far the most traumatic experience of my life. It has made me cold toward everything. You can tell me anything, only death upsets me . . . If you think about everything else in life, everything works itself out. But death doesn't work itself out. Death doesn't get better."[3] The death of his father would affect him for years, and it continues to do so. In many interviews, years apart, he has said he never truly got over it.

He would continue to internalize much of his father's advice, telling Mo Rocca on CBS News how he said, "There's no such thing as early. There's just on time, and late."[4] He credited his father with preventing him from gravitating toward the negative elements in his neighborhood, including the juvenile delinquency that led many of his childhood friends to jail and tragedy.

Aiming for the Big Time

His raw and provocative material and his trademark half-outraged delivery would take Rock beyond the clubs and onto the radar of another influential comedy giant, producer Lorne Michaels. Michaels was famous for creating and running *Saturday Night Live*, the legendary

Live from 30 Rock

The first episode of *Saturday Night Live* premiered in 1975. Performed live before a studio audience, many of its sketches have become pop culture staples. Joining the cast was often a gateway to future success in television and film. Over the years, dozens of talented superstars have written for or performed live for the show from its 30 Rockefeller Center studios.

Rock's mentor and benefactor, Eddie Murphy, was credited with saving the show during a downturn in ratings and quality. Only the show's second African American cast member (Garrett Morris was the first, from 1975 to 1980), Murphy's popularity led to his massively successful Hollywood career.

Among the show's many veterans are actors and writers such as Gilda Radner, Tina Fey, Will Ferrell, Kristen Wiig, Christopher Guest, Julia Louis-Dreyfus, Maya Rudolph, Tracy Morgan, Billy Crystal, Martin Short, Bob Odenkirk, Conan O'Brien, Dana Carvey, Mike Myers, Phil Hartman, and many more.

Arsenio Hall's eponymous late-night talk show was a star-making opportunity for many young African American entertainers in the late 1980s and early 1990s, including Chris Rock.

· · · · · · · · · · · · · · · · · · · ·

live sketch comedy show that broadcast on NBC every Saturday at 11:30 p.m.

In 1990, Rock got word from Michaels's team that he had landed an audition for *SNL*. He partly credited *Comedy's Dirtiest Dozen* for getting him noticed. Buzz surrounding Rock's first national television appearance also helped. Friend and mentor Arsenio Hall had landed a talk show, *The Arsenio Hall Show*, on the then relatively new FOX television network. The show soon became a runaway hit, making waves among young audiences from the MTV generation, especially among hip, urban audiences. Many people were first exposed to Rock's raw brand of humor when he appeared on Hall's show in March 1989.

Rock was excited, but also tense and nervous. It was an audition that could make or break his career. There had not been a black cast member on the show since Damon Wayans and Danitra Vance had left the cast in 1986. While no one expected him to walk in Murphy's footsteps, he nonetheless felt the pressure. He was also still reeling from his father's death. Did he have what it took to be a television star?

Live, from New York—It's Chris Rock!

· · · · · · · · · · · · · · · · · · · ·

While some people might think of comedy as a constant barrel of laughs, many comedians are complicated, often neurotic, competitive, and highly self-critical. In some ways, being slightly "off" is common among most funny people. Stand-up comedy can be a lonely enterprise. Many comedians are road comics, touring much like musicians do all over the country and internationally, from gig to gig. A small minority get top billing in well-paid rooms and sold-out concert halls. Many others scramble to make ends meet. Most who stick it out have a love for the art form, regardless of the monetary gain. However, for those with real talent, like Chris Rock, the fear of failure can be great. There is little worse for a performer than feeling they have squandered their potential. Rock didn't let his fear get the better of him, however.

A Dream Come True

Rock flew to Chicago, joining others for a mass audition. Many performers who audition for *SNL* come from the improv world. Improv, short for improvisation, is a form of theater—including improv comedy—in which the players make up sketches and routines on the spot, without scripts. Others trying out for *SNL* were comic actors or stand-up comics like Rock.

"**Every town has the same two malls: the one white people go to and the one white people used to go to.**"[1]

Another young comic and actor was trying out at the same time: Adam Sandler. Both Sandler and Rock thought their auditions were a toss-up. Their strength was onstage, doing bits and jokes, rather than doing impressions of famous people or entirely made-up characters. Rock finished his audition and headed to his hotel.

Soon, Lorne Michaels invited Rock for a ride in his limousine. After some nervousness driving around with Michaels, it was finally revealed that Rock had made it. He was one of the new cast members, while Sandler would become a writer and eventually perform, too. Chris Farley and Julia Sweeney also came onboard for the 1990–1991 season, while writers Rob Schneider and David Spade became performers.

Michaels often had a gift for casting and had picked Rock, Sandler, and the others for the unique skills and perspectives they would bring to the show. But Rock's casting on the show inspired feelings of both relief and continuing anxiety for the young comic, who was still developing his talent and voice. Still, he later said, "The day I got on *SNL*, I was like, 'Okay, even if I play comedy clubs for the rest of my life, it's a pretty great life.'"[2]

Growing Pains Onstage

He was back in New York to start the 1990 season on *SNL*, but Rock was still anxious. He would be in a very different environment than he had been while working as a stand-up. Though he had experience with show business teamwork, a show like *SNL* was highly

Rock poses with the cast of *Saturday Night Live*. Though frequently frustrating, the experience on *SNL* helped Rock's career and cemented some lifelong friendships.

collaborative. Writers and performers worked together for long hours during the week to get sketches approved for the coming weekend's show and then develop and perfect them. It was far from the independent and solitary work process that stand-ups often employ to perfect their craft.

When he rode up to Harlem with Marci Klein (then a talent associate and now a coproducer of the show) to take promotional pictures for the show's intro, she could tell he was nervous. As she related to *Rolling Stone* in 1997:

> There was a lot of pressure, more than on any cast member I've ever seen come in here, because this is the first black guy—in a long time—to come in since Eddie Murphy, who saved the show during the five years Lorne [Michaels] wasn't here. Now, Lorne's back, and he said, "Chris Rock is funny," and Eddie Murphy said, "Chris Rock is funny," so, OK, be funny. Now we know about comedians—the darkest, most depressed people. Well, Chris is not dark or depressed, but he is a heavy thinker, very sensitive, and extremely hard to get to know. I remember thinking that night, "He is so young"—he would never tell anybody how old he was. I said, "You're scared," and he said, "I'm [expletive] terrified."[3]

While it was a unique opportunity, his time on *SNL* was an altogether mixed bag. A more experienced Rock would later admit that he did not give it his all. Besides the death of his father, it all seemed like too much, too soon. The tightly knit cast would often go out after work many evenings. Rock was far from a drug addict or alcoholic, but there were many late nights where he would show up to work tired from getting only a couple of hours of sleep. He ate poorly, and he found it hard to focus and make a supreme effort on the show. In addition, he sometimes missed rehearsals and occasionally flubbed his lines on air and had to improvise. He told *Rolling Stone* in 2014, "I could've worked harder . . . What I also learned is that there's only a certain amount of hanging out you can do per your talent, and I hung out a little much for the talent I had."[4]

The New (Black) Guy on SNL

Being the sole black performer onstage on *SNL* was both a blessing and a curse. Rock was a perfect comedian for

The Bad Boys of SNL

Rock gravitated toward Sandler and the heavyset, larger-than-life Chris Farley, as well as fellow performers Rob Schneider and David Spade. The group would often work together on each other's sketches and became close friends. All of them would appear in each other's projects for years after they had left *SNL*. Eventually, they became known to comedy fans as the Bad Boys of *SNL*. Unlike some of the older and more experienced veterans of the show, they were known for more juvenile and outlandish behavior, both on and off set. Some people considered some of the Bad Boys' antics "frat boy" comedy. While some found it refreshing, some critics and fans thought the Bad Boys had dumbed down the show with their antics.

the hip-hop generation—and not just black audiences—
because he came of age in the culture. In the 1970s and
1980s, black performers were more often stereotyped
than not, certainly more so than even nowadays.
While Rock's spot on the show allowed him to do some
hilarious social commentary about race relations, as
well as internal divisions and issues affecting African
Americans, it was a delicate balance.

For at least a year before Tim Meadows and Ellen
Cleghorne were hired in 1991, Rock was the show's
only black performer. He was also the new guy, and just

**Rock developed a lasting bond with *SNL* castmates Chris Farley,
Adam Sandler, and David Spade. With the exception of Farley, who
died in 1997, the comedians continue to work together to this day.**

twenty-three years old. Lorne Michaels talked about Rock's progress with the *Los Angeles Times* in 1991: "He's got genuine talent, but he's got some growing to do . . . It takes about a year before most [performers] become familiar enough with how the show works . . . I don't want them to feel as if they have to accomplish everything in six months."[5]

Rock became the show's go-to guy when it came to doing impressions of famous black celebrities, including gently poking fun at his own heroes and friends, Eddie Murphy and Arsenio Hall. Rock also did well-received impressions of Flavor Flav, the hyper rapper from the group Public Enemy, Ugandan dictator Idi Amin, the troubled ex-child actor Todd Bridges, hip-hop pop star MC Hammer, and many others. He also made a mark with multiple segments on the made-up weekly news interlude "Weekend Update," in which he often dropped creative, biting monologues about his life and recent news events.

> I don't believe I can offend you in a comedy club. I don't believe I can offend you in a concert.[6]

In one recurring sketch, Rock played an urban character named Onski, alongside his sidekick B-Fats, on a hip-hop-flavored cable access talk and variety show called *I'm Chillin'*. Another sketch that Rock fronted, "The Dark Side with Nat X," had the comic playing the eponymous militant black nationalist. It was a clever bit because it gave voice to somewhat controversial views and walked a fine line between celebrating and spoofing them.

It was just a sample of the new sensibility of a hip-hop-raised generation on television that would accelerate into the 1990s. Keenen Ivory Wayans's *In Living Color* had debuted earlier in 1990, before Rock was hired on *SNL*, and its candid and provocative sketches featuring a mostly black cast were making waves on the rival FOX network. Meanwhile, *SNL* was struggling to catch up to appeal to a new generation and had been a predominantly white show for most of its run.

Many black performers become weary when they are asked to do the same characters repeatedly because these are the only ones they do because of their skin color. Newcomer Rock sometimes felt like an outsider. "I'm sure I'm the only person on the show to go to Ice Cube and N.W.A. concerts," referring to the "gangsta rap" stars of the era that were blazing up the music charts and challenging mainstream America with tales of the life of the black underclass.

Some things were a bridge too far for Rock when it came to race and performing on *SNL*. He later told podcaster Marc Maron that he would reject sketch ideas such as "[playing] an Ubangi tribesman or whatever. Not that I thought they were racist . . . [but] it feels racist . . . I was the only black face that was going to be seen for an hour and a half. If you're on *In Living Color* and you're a Ubangi tribesman, there was a black thing before that, and one right after it. There's a context."[7]

Rock's fellow cast members could not have been more welcoming and went out of their way to tell media outlets that Rock had been hired for his talent and potential, rather than simply to fill a niche that Michaels feared the show lacked. Still, he felt creatively stumped. Part of the tension arose from the fact that sketches that cast members worked on throughout the week were not guaranteed to make it on air. Often, such decisions were made only a day out from Saturday's performance. As a newcomer, he often had his pet projects axed.

Breaking Through in *New Jack City*

Based on real-life histories of African American crime syndicates in New York and Detroit from the 1970s and 1980s, the film *New Jack City* (1991) made Rock even more of a household name. The gritty, hip, stylized urban drama was directed by Mario Van Peebles and was the hip-hop generation's answer to such classic gangster films like *The Godfather* and *Scarface*.

Rock was thrilled to work alongside stars like Wesley Snipes, rapper-turned-actor Ice-T, Judd Nelson, and a "who's who" cast of leading black talent of the era. He played a recovering drug addict named Pookie, a police informant helping detectives prosecute Snipes's drug kingpin character. Roger Ebert and other movie critics praised Rock's performance, his first truly serious role. He later joked that, as a black man, "I couldn't get a [expletive] cab," but that after the movie came out, "I couldn't take the train either,"[8] due to being recognized so much.

Musician turned actor Ice-T and Rock are shown in a promotional still from the 1991 gangster film *New Jack City*, which allowed Rock to shine in a breakthrough dramatic role.

One Step Back, One Step Forward

After some time, Rock was itching to move on from *SNL*. He told Marc Maron, "I wanted to be in an environment where I didn't have to translate the comedy I wanted to do."[9] He was frustrated that while it was easy enough to get something black-oriented on *SNL*, it was "difficult to get anything black on it that didn't deal specifically with race."[10] He almost left the show in 1992.

Others, like his best friends on the show, Adam Sandler and Chris Farley, had jump-started lucrative comedy film careers with their time on the show. Rock, on the other hand, felt stifled and dead in the water. Besides *New Jack City*, one of his only other projects during his time on SNL had been the Eddie Murphy–helmed comedy *Boomerang*, in which he played a streetwise supporting character named Bony T.

Rock would get his chance in 1993, however. He had appreciated the opportunities Michaels and others had given him. When he went to speak with Michaels about leaving the show, he was thankful that the producer was open-minded. Someone had called and offered Rock a spot on the cast of *In Living Color*. It would be a prominent, leading role. Michaels gave his blessing and "fired" Rock, despite the fact that he still had some time left on his contract. Rock was ecstatic to move on and forward in his career. His new show was at the cutting edge, providing audiences with an unapologetic and often outrageous take on the black experience. He would be in his element.

However, Rock would be in for a rude awakening. While the Wayans family had created the show and made

Brothers Damon Wayans (*left*) and Keenen Ivory Wayans perform in a sketch for *In Living Color*, the landmark predominantly black sketch comedy show that Rock joined at the end of its run.

• • • • • • • • • • • • • • • • • • • •

it a surprise hit, by the last season, Keenen Ivory Wayans and his siblings had largely distanced themselves from the production due to problems with executives at the FOX network. Its days were numbered. The last season, during which Rock joined, had lower ratings and was generally considered worse in quality than prior seasons. Within a few weeks of first getting on the show, *In Living Color* was cancelled, and Chris Rock was out of a job.

Bringing the *Pain*

$\mathbf{R}$ock felt adrift after *SNL* and *In Living Color*. His self-image was perhaps a little too harsh. After all, he had released his first comedy album, *Born Suspect*, in 1991, recorded before an Atlanta, Georgia, audience. He also had a film come out in 1993, *CB4*, a hip-hop comedy spoof of gangsta rap recording artists. Still, it was hardly the wave of project offers and leading roles that fellow *SNL* alumni were enjoying.

Back to the Stage

Despite the feelings of failure and anxiety, Rock decided to go back to his roots and work on his stand-up routines. It is what he considered himself best at, and trying to be famous via film and television gigs seemed to him at best a distraction. Part of him felt somewhat discouraged by his sudden status. He was back working the clubs, but with little to show for it. Rock also had a house now, with bills and a mortgage that required he

A Sleeper Hit: *CB4*

In 1993, Rock was featured as a lead character in *CB4*, a comedy parody about a group of aspiring gangsta rappers mixed up with real criminals. The characters were loosely modeled on recording artists like N.W.A.'s Ice Cube and Dr. Dre. It was Rock's first time working for director Tamra Davis, and it was also a learning opportunity because he cowrote the script with Robert Locash and respected critic, journalist, and filmmaker Nelson George. Its mockumentary style poked fun at the commercialization of ghetto culture and the gangsta rap scene generally. Rock played Albert, aka MC Gusto, who gets into trouble by appropriating the identity and name of a real-life convict, who in turn tries to get revenge on Albert and his friends. Costarring *SNL* Legend Phil Hartman and Rock's *New Jack City* costar Allen Payne, the film became a cult classic and did well financially.

In the 1993 mockumentary *CB4*, Rock played a musician who embraces an over-the-top (and very fake) persona as a gangsta rapper to sell records.

work steadily. He told *Rolling Stone*, "I mean, everything happens for a reason, but when you're in show business, when you ain't working, you're unemployed. You're not 'taking a break,' you are unemployed."[1]

Instead of wallowing in misery, Rock vowed to redouble his efforts to become one of the greatest stand-up comedians of his generation. Much like a boxer who suffers a defeat and goes back to training and watching videos of himself and opponents, Rock absorbed hours upon hours of stand-up from some of his heroes, including videos and seminal comedy albums. He studied up on Richard Pryor, Bill Cosby, Steve Martin, Dick Gregory, and Woody Allen, another hero of his. He aimed to be a great stand-up, versus seeking only fame and success. Rock figured that the latter two things would come once he had perfected the former. One technique he used was breaking down all of the comedic elements he saw in the routines of the legends he so admired: timing, body language, facial expressions, the setup (the lead-up to the payoff), and the punchline, if there even was one.

Besides working on the craft of his comedy routines, he also changed his daily routines. No more would he stay up until all hours and wake up at noon or even one in the afternoon. He started to wake up early and treat stand-up almost as a 9-to-5 job. The comic set up mirrors in a special room in his new home in Brooklyn's Fort Greene neighborhood to better examine his mannerisms and physicality. Outside of the house, he continued playing the clubs, getting his stand-up routine to be leaner, meaner, and funnier.

Another of Rock's formative influences was Richard Pryor, long acknowledged as one of the top ten stand-up comedians of all time. Rock has admitted to studying Pryor's routines to make his own sets better.

While he perfected, Rock landed some commercial spots that kept him in the public eye. The early 1990s were still the era of landlines and pagers, or beepers, and cell phones were not yet widely used. A company called 1-800-Collect—offering a service to save customers long-distance charges using pay phones—enlisted Rock and a couple of his friends, like Arsenio Hall, to star in some advertisementss. Rock even did a voiceover for a puppet version of NBA player Anfernee "Penny" Hardaway in a series of advertisements for Nike, the athletic apparel manufacturer. He beat out Damon Wayans, Martin Lawrence, and other up-and-coming talents for the contract, simultaneously staying on the radar of the hip-hop generation that was his biggest base, while helping him through a career lull.

Don't Call It a Comeback

Cable television had exploded in popularity in the 1990s. Once, late-night talk and variety shows like *The Tonight Show* with Johnny Carson had been the main gatekeepers for stand-up comics to achieve success. Rock had his fair share of stand-up routines on such shows. But cable television and particularly networks like HBO and, later, Comedy Central, shook things up. In this new era, signing up for one or more HBO specials was both a sign that a comedian had made it and also an opportunity to expand his or her audience greatly.

Rock's hard work paid off. He made appearances on the urban-oriented *Def Comedy Jam,* a show launched in part by veteran hip-hop mogul and Def Jam Records cofounder Russell Simmons. He also performed for the debut of the *HBO Comedy Half-Hour* special, which premiered in June 1994. However, his bigger triumph from this era was broadcasting his own HBO comedy special, *Big A** Jokes*. It was hardly the breakthrough that he had hoped for, and it got somewhat mixed reviews, but it marked Rock's return to the comedy scene in a big way. He was back on the map.

The following two years saw Rock steadily employed, even as he continued fine-tuning his stand-up chops. He did voiceover work for an animated series on the Cartoon Network called *The Moxy Show* and made cameo guest appearances on the hit sitcoms *The Fresh Prince of Bel-Air* and *Martin*, fellow comic Martin Lawrence's star vehicle. He even did a dramatic turn, guest starring on an episode of *Homicide: Life on the Street*. All this was only a prelude to all the success, fame, and notoriety a new stand-up special on HBO would unlock for Chris Rock, however.

A Career-Making Turn: *Bring the Pain*

Show business can often be a series of ups and downs, even for very talented performers. After two years of perfecting new routines, Rock was hungry for the spotlight and to prove his mettle to audiences. Writer Nelson George told *Rolling Stone* that his friend prepared extensively for a national tour by getting onstage somewhere, saying, "he trained like a fighter. For a few months, every single night—leaving the house at about nine and coming in at about two."[2]

During his tour, it was decided that the production team film the HBO special specifically at a small, more intimate theater, the Takoma, in Washington, DC, where the audience would heavily skew African American, to provide the biggest potential positive feedback from a sympathetic audience. Even so, Rock was a little nervous since the producers even had to give away some tickets to make sure it was a packed house. The producing/directing team of Keith Truesdell and Sandy Chanley had done Rock's earlier *Big A** Jokes*. Chanley got a sneak peek at some the material that Rock was workshopping for the tour at the Comedy Store in Los Angeles and was amazed and floored by the change in Rock. "I'd pop in to see him, and he'd just have this little notepad on the stool next to him," Chanley told Yahoo! Entertainment. "Sitting there listening to what he was about to lay down on an uncensored network, [I knew] it was going to be a breakthrough."[3]

When they filmed the performance, everyone knew they had something special on their hands. The jokes were raw, bold, insightful, and, above all, hilarious. Rock skewered many sacred idols and tackled everything from racism and race relations, to relationships, family life, parenting, the controversial O. J. Simpson murder case, drugs and crime, and much more. With his aggressive, loud, and expressive delivery, Rock seemed to stalk the stage like a panther.

The audience response was tremendous, and when *Chris Rock: Bring the Pain* was broadcast in June 1996, word of mouth exploded over the groundbreaking and controversial special. Some of the racier material dealt with internal contradictions within the black community itself, and more than a few cultural commentators

The 1996 broadcast of Rock's comedy tour *Bring the Pain* expanded the comedian's audience and took his career to the next level. Many consider the show to be Rock's seminal work.

accused Rock of "airing the dirty laundry" of the black community. Far more deemed the show an instant classic, and the reviews and acclaim had some calling Rock the rightful heir to the legacy of Cosby, Pryor, and Murphy himself.

Two years earlier, Rock had felt like he was starting over at the bottom of the comedy game, and *Bring the Pain* now became his ticket back. Even Rock was surprised at how much of an impact it had. When it came out, and in the years following, it was recognized as an iconic, star-making performance, and it rejuvenated his career. For a newer generation, it was as important as Eddie Murphy's *Delirious* and *Raw* specials, Bill Cosby's *Himself*, or Steve Martin's *A Wild and Crazy Guy*. While Rock had some high hopes for the special—perhaps a sitcom offer, or at least more specials from HBO or other networks and producers—its success and impact exceeded his wildest dreams.

During the 1997 Emmy Awards, which recognize excellence in primetime television programming, *Bring the Pain* won not one, but two Emmys: Outstanding Writing for a Variety or Music Program and Outstanding Variety, Music, or Comedy Special. Rock was even competing against himself that year. He had also been nominated for a well-received stint covering the 1996 election season as a cynically funny roving correspondent for the Comedy Central political talk show *Politically Incorrect with Bill Maher*. That award, Outstanding Writer for a Variety or Music Program, was earned alongside his fellow winners, the show's larger writing staff.

Chris Rock on . . . Everything

Never shying from controversy, Rock has been praised for "telling it like it is." Some observations from his stand-up follow:

From *Bring the Pain*:

"Who's more racist? Black people or white people? Black people. You know why? 'Cuz we hate black people, too!"

"Everybody is talking about gun control . . . No, I think we need some bullet control. I think every bullet should cost five thousand dollars. Five thousand dollars for a bullet. Know why? 'Cause if a bullet cost five thousand dollars, there'd be no more innocent bystanders!"[4]

From *Never Scared*:

"America is the only place where people go hunting on a full stomach!"

"Are we so desperate for entertainment that we fall for a trickless magician? Saw a lady in half. Pull a rabbit out of a hat. Do something. What's his last trick? 'I'm in a box and I ain't going to eat.' That ain't no trick. That's called living in the projects."[5]

The *Chris Rock Show* debuted in 1997 and ran for several seasons, helping Rock make his own unique mark on late-night television.

• •

Coasting along on the success of the HBO performance, he took some of the same material and combined it with other bits to put out 1997's *Roll with the New*, his second comedy album. This is turn earned him an Emmy in 1998 for Best Spoken Comedy Album.

Killing It on Cable: *The Chris Rock Show*

The popularity and quality of his special would start to unlock new and bigger opportunities for Rock. Striking while the iron was hot, Rock warmed to an offer from HBO. They offered him his own comedic talk show with a great deal of creative control, dubbed *The Chris Rock Show*. As with his specials, broadcasting on HBO also meant Rock would have more leeway when it came to using profanity, doing risqué humor, and generally pushing the creative envelope. It was yet another lifelong ambition fulfilled that many other comedians would have eagerly embraced.

The lucrative HBO deal included budgets for writers and other staff. Rock's production team consisted of about thirty people with offices in New York City's Midtown. Two of the head writers that helped Rock were comedians Wanda Sykes and Louis C.K., who later collaborated with him on other projects. One of Rock's biggest pleasures was working creatively with other writers, especially friends whose stand-up and humor he appreciated.

> "You don't need a critic to tell you people aren't laughing."[6]

The Chris Rock Show hosted guests from the worlds of entertainment and politics, including comedians, activists, musicians, and other luminaries. The first episode premiered in February 1997. Lawyer Johnnie Cochran, who had helped exonerate O. J. Simpson in the famous murder trial, was the first guest interview, with Prince as musical guest. Its sketches satirized many modern issues. As *Variety* pointed out in its review of the debut episode, Chris Rock "has charisma and attitude to burn, and this offbeat format plays well to Rock's strengths."[7]

Though he had complicated feelings about his stint on *SNL*, one thing his time on the show had helped him with was figuring out how to bring a sketch or other production from idea to execution—including writing, rehearsing, costumes, scenery, and everything else. If nothing else, *SNL* had provided a comprehensive training ground.

The show garnered excellent reviews all around, becoming a critical and audience favorite. Rock and his writers shared an Emmy in 1999 for Outstanding Writing for a Variety or Music Program. The show also earned accolades from the American Comedy Awards and a National Association for the Advancement of Colored People (NAACP)'s Image Award.

At the Top of His Game

C hris Rock was finally in a place where he felt he could call the shots. His HBO talk show ran for fifty-five episodes over five seasons. The show's creative force decided to call it quits himself. Some of his best writers, including Louis C.K. and Wanda Sykes, had moved on to other projects as their own careers took off. Once he had a roomful of writers and realized he barely recognized half of them, he decided it was time to put the show to rest. He has always expressed interest in doing another talk show, as long as he can recruit close, talented friends.

Rocking Hollywood

His hosting duties, stand-up tours, and specials kept Rock busy. Soon, the television star would turn more of his attention to the big screen and expand his horizons— not simply acting, but screenwriting, producing, and directing as well. He had fit some movie parts into his

A Master of Ceremonies

One sign of having "made it" in show business is being selected as an awards host. Supremely confident onstage, and now a seasoned producer and television host, it was only natural that big telecasts would come calling for Rock as an emcee. The first major hosting gig he took was for the 1997 MTV Video Music Awards, when the video and reality network was seemingly at its prime. He returned again in 1999 and 2003 for some of the show's most memorable broadcasts. He joked to *The A.V. Club*, "I like the MTV Awards, because you're hip by association. It's like, 'Okay, I'm here, so I must be hip, since I'm next to all the hip people.'"[1]

Partly due to his MTV achievements, he was also picked to host an even more prestigious event, the 77th Academy Awards, in 2005. He even returned in 2016, making him one of several other big stars, including Ellen DeGeneres, Jon Stewart, and Richard Pryor, among others, to host the show more than once.

schedule in the late 1990s while his main "day job" had been his talk show. He teamed up with Steve Martin and fellow *SNL* costar Phil Hartman in the military comedy *Sgt. Bilko* in 1996, appeared with good friend Chris Farley in 1997's *Beverly Hills Ninja*, and voiced a guinea pig, alongside Eddie Murphy as the title character, in *Dr. Doolittle*, released in 1998.

One major role that literally let Rock spread his comedic wings was as an actual angel. Director Kevin Smith assembled actors Matt Damon and Ben Affleck,

Rock has proven to be a popular and innovative awards show host. During the 2016 Academy Awards ceremony, he brought out Girl Scouts to sell cookies to the hungry audience of Hollywood stars.

• •

along with comedians like Janeane Garofalo, George Carlin, and Rock in 1999 in a biblically themed fantasy comedy about faith called *Dogma*. Rock played Rufus, an angel and the missing thirteenth apostle of Jesus Christ. He followed it up with a major role as a wisecracking hitman in 2000's *Nurse Betty*, playing opposite Morgan Freeman and Renée Zellweger.

Religion would also figure heavily in the fantasy comedy *Down to Earth* (2001), in which Rock had a leading role as Lance Barton, a struggling comedian who is killed before his time on Earth is up and is brought back to life in the body of a wealthy, middle-aged white man. Louis C.K., Ali LeRoi, and Lance Crouther—all writers on *The Chris Rock Show*—were involved with *Down to Earth* and would soon work with Rock again on another film that both elevated and mocked blaxploitation tropes, *Pootie Tang*, in 2001. Around this time, Rock also costarred with Anthony Hopkins in the 2002 action buddy comedy *Bad Company*, did the voice for the title character in the animated comedy adventure *Osmosis Jones* (2001), and appeared in *Comedian* (2002), a documentary about colleague and friend Jerry Seinfeld.

> "Yeah, I love being famous. It's almost like being white, y'know."[2]

Chris Rock, First Black President

In his stand-up, Chris Rock often joked about how both blacks and whites might react to the first black president. Rock went out on a professional limb in 2003, when he made his directorial debut, cowriting with Ali LeRoi the film *Head of State*. It tells the tale of Mays Gilliam, a minor Washington, DC, politician who becomes a hero during an accident that claims the lives of a presidential candidate and his running mate. Soon, Gilliam is enlisted to run for president. Set up to lose by his own party, he gains popularity by speaking plainly and truthfully about controversial issues and picks a bail bondsman as his running mate, played by Bernie Mac. While *Head*

Rock costarred as an apostle in the Kevin Smith 1999 film *Dogma* alongside Jason Mewes and Salma Hayek.

• •

of State got mixed reviews, critic Roger Ebert declared it "an imperfect movie, but not a boring one and not lacking in intelligence."[3]

Rock had found inspiration for doing the film from several past experiences. One of these was his coverage of the 1996 presidential campaign for *Politically Incorrect*. Another was his opinion about the 1984 presidential election, in which Senator Walter Mondale picked Congresswoman Geraldine Ferraro as a running mate, which Rock thought was a good way to push for women's rights, even if everyone thought they would eventually lose to Ronald Reagan, as they did. Part of the reason he claimed to have decided to direct *Head of State* himself was that it was easier to shop it around with a big name already attached. Rock was also inspired by the example of his old hero, Woody Allen, who had done stand-up and acted in addition to directing. The film was praised for pointing out how election campaigns had become spectacles where real human needs and issues were ignored in favor of star power and gossip. Ultimately, however, Rock waved away any hopes of making political points, reminding interviewers that his primary goal was to make audiences laugh.

Bigger & Blacker, but Never Scared

At the turn of the millennium, Rock was eager to show he still had it onstage. While his groundbreaking *Bring the Pain* would be a hard act to follow, many critics praised Rock's comeback to the stage. He filmed *Bigger & Blacker* in June 1999 at Harlem's famous Apollo Theater. He seemed to have kept the manic and raucous delivery and smart, cutting material that made him famous. A few years later, comedy fans and critics both seemed to agree that he had not lost his edge, even if his stand-up formula remained largely the same, in 2004's *Never Scared*. Nevertheless, Rock kept up with the times, always ripping inspired bits from modern headlines and challenging his audiences. Even if they thought he took some jokes too far, he rarely did so without leaving them in stitches.

Rock examined his childhood in the popular television sitcom *Everybody Hates Chris*. Here he gives direction to actor Tyler James Williams, who played a fictional version of the young Rock.

Everybody Hates Chris

Some of Rock's projects had found critical acclaim, while others were perhaps only essential to his biggest fans. With several HBO specials, a talk show, and a film under his belt, he turned his attention back to television, with the end result being one of his most personal projects yet. With longtime collaborator Ali LeRoi, Rock set out to do a sitcom based heavily on his own youth. Spoofing the title of hit sitcom *Everybody Loves Raymond*, the show was called *Everybody Hates Chris*, and it premiered in September 2002 on the UPN network, later rebranded as part of The CW.

Starring Tyler James Williams as the title character based on Rock's own youthful self, the show switched the original setting of Rock's preteen and teenage years from the late 1970s to the period spanning 1982 through 1987. The Bedford-Stuyvesant setting remained the same, however. Father Julius, based on Rock's real dad, was played by Terry Crews, while mother Rose became known as Rochelle onscreen and was portrayed by actress Tichina Arnold. Chris's exploits at home and school were chronicled by a voiceover done by Rock himself. His hectic home life, loving family, and experiences with racism at school were dealt with comically rather than in a heavy, dramatic fashion. The show was also a way for Rock to both humorously honor his upbringing—especially his late father—and provide a nostalgic but witty snapshot of a different time, when no-nonsense, disciplinarian parents were the norm.

Running for four seasons from 2005 through 2009, *Everybody Hates Chris* received many nominations for the NAACP Image Awards and Teen Choice Awards for its cast members and a Golden Globe nomination in 2006 for Best Television Series (Musical or Comedy), amid other accolades. Waning ratings toward the end, and Rock's wish to end the series just shy of the main character leaving high school and becoming a stand-up comedian, were two of the reasons that the show ended its run. The American Film Institute declared the sitcom among the ten best television series of 2007, praising it as both realistic and timely, as well as original in its ways of portraying race and class onscreen. Audiences

Rock found himself in front of the camera for the 2003 political comedy *Head of State*, as well as behind it, for his directorial debut.

seemed to agree, and Rock was pleased that they did so while seeing the show as not jut a black sitcom, but one that could appeal to anyone.

Leading Man Material

During his sitcom run, Rock also kept busy in the film world. Again, he called upon a frequent writing partner and cowrote *I Think I Love My Wife*, a romantic comedy with Rock in the lead role as a man tempted to cheat on his wife, played by Gina Torres, with an old friend, portrayed by Kerry Washington. Rock once again stepped into the director's chair and coproduced the film as well, which was a loose remake of a 1972 French film, *Love in the Afternoon*.

In an interview session with film criticism site Collider, Rock joked about how directing and producing the film was the only way he could get such a film made with him as a leading man. He said, "I wanted to have a departure. I wanted to be a grownup in a movie. No one was ever going to cast me in a part like this. It was never going to happen. So, I really wanted to play a grown man and I still wanted it to be really funny. There is like this thought that if you do something mature, it's not going to be as funny as the gross out stuff. And I was like, 'No man, we are going to play a grown man and it's going to be real funny with grown man problems.'"[4]

Rock also admitted that he still had a lot to learn about directing. Rather than letting the jokes carry the film, he hoped that the story and performances would give the movie more depth and feeling than, say, *Head of State* had. Some critics praised the extra effort, such as

A. O. Scott in the *New York Times*, who thought that the film cleverly bridged two genres: the innovative French New Wave cinema of the 1960s and African American romantic comedies of the 1990s and 2000s. Scott wrote, "Rock has not only done his best work so far as a director and a screenwriter, but he has also made an unusually insightful and funny mainstream American movie about the predicaments of modern marriage."[5]

"Sit Back and Relax": *Good Hair*

Rock was always ready to try new things and push the envelope. He approached writer, producer, and fellow stand-up comic Jeff Stilson, a veteran of *The Chris Rock Show*, with an idea. Rock's daughter had asked him, "Daddy, why don't I have good hair?" Aghast at the idea that his daughter could be ashamed of her hair, Rock was inspired to do a documentary about black women and their hairstyling habits. Cowritten by Stilson, Chuck Sklar, and Lance Crouther, *Good Hair*, released in 2009, featured Rock visiting hair salons and engaging both hairstylists and customers, interviewing in his typical up-front and everyman fashion. A host of other African American celebrities chimed in, too, including Nia Long, Raven-Symoné, T-Pain, Ice-T, Kerry Washington, Eve, and many more.

Film critic Roger Ebert praised Rock's narration and interviewing skills in his review of the film. He called Rock "a likable man, truly curious, with the gift of encouraging people to speak openly about a subject they usually keep private."[6] Other critics agreed, and the film won Special Jury Prize at the Sundance Film Festival in Park City, Utah, that year.

Rock thought it was important to uncover both the fascinating and little-discussed aspects of black people's self-image and the billion-dollar black hair-care industry. Nia Long agreed, telling the *Los Angeles Times* in October 2009, "Hair is such a taboo subject in the black community . . . And I know personally how important hair on black women in show business is."[7] Once more, Rock was going where others were unlikely to tread and doing it in entertaining and thought-provoking ways.

A Cut Above
the Rest

· · · · · · · · · · · · ·

A s the 2000s came to a close, Chris Rock could look back at ten years of accomplishments he could be proud of. In 2008, his last stand-up special, and his fifth for HBO, had been entitled *Kill the Messenger*, again underscoring that audiences should be ready for some uncomfortable—albeit funny—truths and observations. It would be quite a number of years before he returned to the comedy stage for another one, and he would not tour for the better part of a decade.

A Different Kind of Stage

Rock got up on an entirely different kind of stage in 2007. As part of a charity event, the Urban Arts Partnership invited Rock and other actors to do original ten-minute plays. The catch was that each had to be written and rehearsed with only twenty-four hours of lead time. The process proved nerve-wracking for Rock, but he was intrigued by the experience. It would inspire him to push himself even further four years later, when he made his Broadway debut in 2011 at the not-so-tender age of forty-six.

Written by Stephen Adly Guirgis and directed by Anna D. Shapiro *The _____ with the Hat* was an even wider departure from Rock's already expanded comfort zone. The play was not too far removed, however, from the seedier environments he had explored in films like *New Jack City*. Rock played Ralph D., a twelve-step sponsor (someone who helps another person stay sober) who is involved in a love triangle with a couple of drug addicts. Rock told the *New York Times* that the play was

Fellow cast members—including (*from left*) Annabella Sciorra, Bobby Cannavale, Elizabeth Rodriguez, and Yul Vazquez—join Rock onstage for the curtain call of the play, *The _____ with the Hat*.

so good that he just wanted to be involved. "'You can't play the lead. Not a lot of money. You have to read for it' . . . I'm like: 'I don't care. I hadn't seen anything [so] good in so long.'"[1]

Rock saw the play as an opportunity to show a different side of himself and slow down somewhat from the usual frantic pace and rapid-fire delivery of his stand-up performances. Shapiro, the director, noted how differently Rock had to approach the material: "He paces the stage like a puma . . . Now he's learning to take that wide focus and make it a laser focus. He's learning that the most important person onstage is his partner."[2]

Movies have takes. But plays are like life—you don't really get takes. [3]

It was an entirely different kind of time commitment, too, in that he would perform for a four-month run. Being onstage in this new manner, night after night, also served to change his perspective of—and opinions about—the theater. Though Rock had not dreamed of doing theater as a child, like many actors and even comedians do, he found that doing it gave him a newfound respect for both actors and others in theater production, and for himself. Rock freely admitted that he could not have gotten through the ordeal of theater years earlier, due to being more impatient and cocky during that time. Luckily, he had his *SNL* experiences to draw on, which armed him better for the theater experience than film or comedy had. In turn, he felt the play made him a better actor. He told *Rolling Stone*:

The play taught me that I could work harder and that there was something to get out of working harder. I remember in school, once you realize you're not going to be an A student, you realize that the A's get treated differently, but B and D are all the same. There is no difference in the treatment of a B student and a D student. Nothing! So there might've been a little bit of that in my career—I'm OK, I'll get work. When I got in the play, I was literally working with the best people in the world.[4]

Returning to *SNL*

Many stand-up comedians enjoy hosting *SNL* because they also get to do an opening monologue, which many are happy to use to promote their most recent and upcoming projects. Rock has made a couple of returns to the show. The first one was on November 2, 1996, and it served as Rock's victory lap after *Bring the Pain* blew up. Hosting the show seemed to suit him better than his earlier stint doing sketches.

His other *SNL* hosting gig aired November 1, 2014. Rock pushed the envelope a little bit too far for some, due to a few jokes involving the 9/11 attacks and the more recent bombing at the Boston Marathon. Others praised him for tackling sensitive material and thought the resulting social media backlash was an overreaction. Rock himself has said that people are far too easily offended these days, and he even quit touring colleges partly due to what he felt were oversensitive audiences.

Back on the Silver Screen

Rock's face was largely absent from movie screens in the late 2000s. Besides a cameo role in his friend Adam Sandler's 2008 film, *You Don't Mess with the Zohan*, his biggest roles around this time were animated voiceovers. In *Madagascar* (2005) and its sequel, *Madagascar: Escape 2 Africa* (2008), Rock lent his voice and comic relief support to the character of Marty, a cartoon zebra, alongside fellow voice actors Ben Stiller, David Schwimmer, and Jada Pinkett Smith. In 2007, he took a voice acting gig in another DreamWorks animated project, *Bee Movie*. Rock was part of a supporting cast that included his friend Jerry Seinfeld in the lead role,

Rock joins fellow *Madagascar* cast members David Schwimmer, Jada Pinkett Smith, and Ben Stiller for the film's 2005 New York premiere. Each actor held a stuffed animal of the character they voiced in the film.

along with former *Nurse Betty* cast member Renée Zellweger.

Next up for Rock was the 2010 ensemble comedy *Death at a Funeral*, in which he costarred with Martin Lawrence as brothers dealing with various hijinks of family and friends following the funeral of their father. As one of the producers on the film, Rock was particularly happy to persuade longtime friend Lawrence to come onboard. The two comedians had not performed in a project together since 1992's *Boomerang* and had traded scripts for years to try to make it finally happen. Since it was based on a 2007 British film, Rock observed that it was easy to attract some good actors to the remake, including Tracy Morgan, Zoe Saldana, and Peter Dinklage. The film's slapstick and screwball humor earned it its fair share of comedy fans, many of whom compared it favorably with the original.

That same year, Rock reunited on the big screen with fellow *SNL* Bad Boys and real-life friends Adam Sandler, David Spade, and Rob Schneider for the Sandler-produced *Grown Ups*. Other alumni of the comedy sketch series, including Tim Meadows, Colin Quinn, Maya Rudolph, and Norm Macdonald, rounded out the cast. Like many movies Rock and the other actors were doing around this time, it lampooned the middle age that all the actors were experiencing.

2 Days in New York

Still, it seemed inevitable that Rock would once again gravitate to more nuanced and well-rounded roles. Turning away from juvenile humor, he soon tackled

Longtime friends and colleagues Chris Rock and Jerry Seinfeld are both known for their exacting approaches to the craft of stand-up comedy.

another kind of comedy. French actress and director Julie Delpy had cowritten a romantic comedy, entitled *2 Days in New York*, a sequel to her 2007 film, *2 Days in Paris*, and was set to direct and produce it. Rock was Delpy's first pick for a leading man. His only requirement when he was first asked was that the script not be "really, really bad," according to an interview Delpy and Rock did for the *Huffington Post*.[5] He actually loved the script, which he read in an hour, and agreed to do it almost immediately.

Part of the fun for Rock was working around the language barrier, since many of the lines are delivered in French. "It worked because my character didn't speak

Runs in the Family

From his grandfather's humor to his father's wit to Rock's own success as a comedian, it seems that talent runs in the family. Inspired by Chris, his brothers Jordan, nearly half Chris's age at twenty-six, and Tony, ten years his junior, are pursuing their own comedy careers. Naturally, one of the hardest parts of pursuing a career in the shadow of one's megastar brother is carving out one's own path and niche. A famous name can be both a blessing and a curse. Tony Rock has done well, hosting *All Def Comedy* on HBO (a successor to the earlier *Def Comedy Jam*), taping a recent pilot sitcom for CBS, and touring comedy clubs regularly. Meanwhile, Jordan Rock, considered the baby of the family, is still making his bones and just landed a spot on the Netflix show *Love*.

French in the movie, so I didn't have to act confused—I was really confused. I think at one point it looked like I was looking down at the subtitles," he joked. The film also worked on another level since it portrayed a dysfunctional relationship, of which Rock said, "I've had dysfunctional relationships with all sorts of women."[6]

In the film, Rock and Delpy's characters, talk-radio host Mingus and photographer Marion, are both single parents of very young children, all happily living together—that is, until Delpy's family barges into their lives during a trip across the Atlantic Ocean. While Delpy's Marion and her family are eccentric and somewhat crazy, Roger Ebert pointed out in his review of the film that Rock is "the most stable and sane member of the cast" whose main refuge, nonetheless, "is to retreat into his man cave and have thoughtful conversations with a life-sized cardboard cutout of Barack Obama."[7]

A Creative Breakthrough: *Top Five*

Continuing a journey from *SNL* Bad Boy to well-regarded filmmaker, the next project Rock embraced would demonstrate even more maturity and professionalism. The second decade of the twenty-first century has been widely praised as a new golden era of television—not just for the many dramas receiving critical acclaim, but also for fresh voices in half-hour comedy. Rock's friend and frequent collaborator (before taking a leave of absence in 2017 due to reported sexual improprieties) Louis C.K. produced *Louie*, a television show for FX in which the comedian plays a realistic but fictional version of himself.

In 2014's *Top Five*, featuring a cast of luminaries including Gabrielle Union, Rock took even greater creative risks as a director.

• •

A similar show was *Seinfeld* creator Larry David's *Curb Your Enthusiasm* on HBO.

Rock was intrigued by the possibilities such shows and their unique voices could bring if translated to the big screen. He told *Rolling Stone*, "I watch *Louie, Seinfeld, Curb Your Enthusiasm*. I thought, 'Let's do a movie like that, but about the whole idea of black fame.' I wanted to make a nuanced black movie."[8] Rock was tired of black-helmed films where the rich or educated characters were always the bad guys or where black characters were expected to act like saints and be a model for others' behavior. Black people were always expected to do something for the community through their portrayals, he felt. Rock quipped, "No one's mad at [Maroon 5 singer] Adam Levine—'What are you doing for people with great haircuts?'"[9]

The result was *Top Five*, released in December 2014. In it, Rock plays the lead role of Andre Allen, a recovering alcoholic and comedian, very loosely based on Rock's own persona. Like *Curb Your Enthusiasm*, the film is enriched with cameos by actors who play versions of their real selves, including Jerry Seinfeld, Whoopi Goldberg, Luis Guzman, Adam Sandler, Taraji P. Henson, Gabourey Sidibe, and even rapper DMX. Comedians like Leslie Jones, Tracy Morgan, Kevin Hart, Cedric the Entertainer, and JB Smoove round out the cast in fictional roles. Leading lady Rosario Dawson plays a reporter assigned to cover Andre and becomes his unlikely romantic interest in the film, with her main goal being figuring out why the comic has suffered a career slump.

Critics generally praised the chemistry between Rock and Dawson, with *Denver Post* writer Lisa Kennedy noting that "the pair's walking and talking, limousine-riding and back-seat gabbing allows them to entertain funny as well as funny-sad theories about comedy and sobriety, fakery and authenticity, celebrity and creativity."[10] The film allowed Rock to tread a delicate balance between comedy and tragedy, providing him with a new creative terrain.

Allen's tale also seemed a stand-in for Rock's own feelings about his career. As *St. Louis Post-Dispatch* critic Calvin Wilson noted about the lead character, famous as one half of a buddy-cop team, "Andre, a once-edgy comedian who's gone Hollywood, views the character as a waste of his talent."[11] Wilson added that this, the third film that Rock wrote and directed, "was one of the best comedies of the year. His newfound confidence behind the camera is at once exhilarating and reminiscent of Woody Allen at his best (the lead character's surname is probably no coincidence)."[12] Rock had long idolized Allen creatively and was probably greatly pleased by the comparison.

Up Close and Personal

● ● ● ● ● ● ● ● ● ● ● ● ●

Chris Rock credits his parents and family for giving him the necessary life tools to achieve success. Much of his material onstage comes from personal experiences. To get a deeper sense of Chris Rock the performer, beyond his incredible success on the comedy stage, on television, and in films, it is necessary to explore Rock as a human being, friend, and family man.

Love and Marriage

In 1994, Rock and a few friends attended a party honoring the *Essence* Awards, an annual event held by the black-targeted lifestyle magazine. It was there that he met Malaak Compton, a public relations professional. Raised in Oakland, California, Compton earned a degree in arts management from Howard University, one of the most respected historically black universities. At the time, she worked for the United Nations Children's Fund (UNICEF), and once they started dating, one or the

Chris Rock met Malaak Compton in 1994, marrying the public relations professional two years later.

other of them would travel cross-country since she was always traveling for work and Rock was always shooting somewhere. They married on November 23, 1996, after about two years of dating.

In May 1997, Rock told *Ebony* magazine about how domestic life came as a blessing to him, helping to ground him. "She's changed me. We've been together for three years . . . She's really calmed me down and centered my life. I'm not running around, chasing women like I used to. I get more work done. She's really centered me."[1]

Malaak Compton-Rock: Giving Back

Malaak Compton-Rock was dedicated to the nonprofit sector. After working for UNICEF she began Styleworks, a nonprofit organization in Brooklyn that helped newly divorced and formerly incarcerated women transition back to the workforce and financial independence. The main services Styleworks provided were hairstyling, makeup, and skin care for women in financial need so that they could more easily and confidently look for work, as well as maintain a professional demeanor when dealing with parole and other government officials. Compton-Rock also launched a website, the Angel Rock Project, which tied together various projects and philanthropic efforts she coordinated, many made possible by her own and her husband's connections in the celebrity world. Compton-Rock also befriended media mogul Oprah Winfrey, appeared on her show three times, and attended the opening of a school Winfrey opened in South Africa.

One thing that appealed to Compton about Rock was his closeness with his family, which came out especially when Chris and his brothers talked about their father. She told *Rolling Stone*, "I feel like I know his father. I don't think a day goes by that one of the brothers is not telling a story about his dad. He and his brothers Andre and Tony are just incredibly tight. Their dad stressed togetherness, and they're just really beautiful together."[2]

A New Generation of Rocks

During the first few years of their marriage, while Rock was occupied with his talk show and other projects, he declared that he wanted to hold off on having children. He felt too busy to commit to fatherhood and wanted to be able to give any kids his full attention when he felt the time was right. For a while, the couple lived more or less happily in a converted three-story carriage house in Brooklyn's Clinton Hill neighborhood.

However, circumstances often change. It was the tragedy of September 11, 2001, when thousands were killed in the al-Qaeda terrorist attacks, that made Rock step back and review his priorities. He told Oprah Winfrey in 2002, "I said to myself, 'The world's falling down, and what have I done with my life?' We've been married five years, but we've never planned anything—it has always been about today. After September 11, I said, 'It's time to have a baby.'"[3]

Rock and his wife welcomed Lola Simone Rock into the world on June 28, 2002, just about nine months after 9/11. The new father admitted that he would have loved a boy just as much but that he feared he would have been too hard on a male child. Rock looked forward to "not being tired around my child," he informed Winfrey. "My father was tired a lot," he admitted, due to working so hard. Rock's wealth and lifestyle seemed like they would allow him much more free time with his daughter.[4]

When Lola Simone was just shy of two years old, her parents had a second child, Zahra Savannah Rock, born on May 22, 2004. Needless to say, fatherhood and raising children were a far cry from the world of entertainment. Feeding, changing, and helping babies and toddlers learn about the world around them required a whole different skill set. Parenthood can also throw many curve balls, especially at new parents. Young Zahra had an asthma scare early on as a toddler, along with a peanut allergy.

As his daughters have grown into teenagers, he has applied some lessons from his own upbringing—but not all. He told WebMd, "I try to be strict. But the circumstances aren't as grave. I grew up in the 'hood! Paying attention to authority was very important to my parents."[5] Years before, he had moved out of Brooklyn into a mansion in Alpine, New Jersey, a short drive across the Hudson to New York City. The girls had grown up in the suburbs. More importantly, they were growing up in an entirely different era than his youth. A sterner upbringing, like the one his own parents gave him, would not fit his daughters' circumstances. Meanwhile, as he told interviewer Mo Rocca, "My father was saving me from going to jail."[6]

Rock realizes that he is lucky to have the resources and flexibility to spend a great deal of time with his children. He knows that not all parents in his industry—or parents

in general—feel the same way. He told National Public
Radio in 2012:

> I never really looked at it [raising kids] as a chore or
> whatever. When I hear people talk about juggling or the
> sacrifices they make for their children, I look at them
> like they're crazy because "sacrifice" infers that there

**Proud father Chris Rock posed for the cameras with daughters Lola
Simone Rock (*left*) and Zahra Savannah Rock during an outing in
June 2008.**

was something better to do than the thing—than being with your children. I've never been with my kids and go, "Man, I wish I was onstage right now" [or] "It would be so great if I was on a movie set right now." But I've been doing a movie and wished that I was with my kids. I've been on tour and wished I was with my kids. It's like being with my kids is like the best, most fun thing. You know, it's a privilege. It is not something I call a sacrifice.[7]

Trouble in Paradise

Rock and his wife were married for years. On the surface, things seemed mostly fine. They had two daughters and even adopted Ntombi-futhi Samantha, an infant girl from South Africa, in 2008. Out of the public eye, however, they were going through some rocky times. In 2004, Rock revealed to radio host Howard Stern that he had been unfaithful with a woman in 1998, during a time when he and his wife were briefly separated. The woman later sued Rock, claiming he had fathered a child she bore, but a paternity test revealed Rock was not the father. Rock told Stern that he and his wife had worked things out and decided to remain together after the incident. While rumors surfaced in 2006 that Rock and Compton-Rock might divorce, the couple issued press releases denying that would be the case.

> "Being with my kids is like the best, most fun thing. You know, it's a privilege."

90

However, within another ten years' time, things had hit the breaking point. Rock later admitted that he had again been unfaithful several more times, with as many as three different women. Multiple news outlets reported in 2014 that Rock and Malaak Compton-Rock would be going their separate ways and filing for divorce. The decision, Rock says, was ultimately his, as he realized they had grown too far apart to save their marriage.

The next few years were very difficult for the family. Aside from the guilt he felt—Rock admitted that, for various reasons, he was largely to blame for a growing

Don't Go There

Over time, Rock has established ground rules on what he will and won't joke about onstage or incorporate into scripts. One of these topics is God. Religion may provide Rock with comic fodder, but directly attacking or criticizing the deity is a no-no for him. He has always felt it would be a sign of disrespect, especially against his dearly departed preacher grandfather.

In addition, Rock has steered clear of jokes about senility or Alzheimer's disease, mainly because he once revealed that his grandmother suffered from dementia. Eventually, she had troubling recognizing her family.

He also goes out of his way to avoid referencing actual personal events or exposing his family to any undue and unfair attention. At the very least, he makes it clear that while some of his stand-up is based on his life, that does not necessarily mean he personally experiences everything he talks about.

rift between himself and his wife—they spent a long time finalizing the terms of the divorce. This included fighting over details dealing with custody and visitation of their daughters and figuring out how to split their financial assets. To add insult to injury, while the divorce was being negotiated, Rose Rock fell ill. His mother had been diagnosed with cancer and was undergoing treatment at Memorial Sloan-Kettering Cancer Center. The center happened to be on the same street as Rock's divorce attorney, an unwelcome reminder to Rock that when problems rained down in life, they often poured. Luckily, his mother fought back and recovered from the disease.

Ultimately, the unhappy ex-couple ironed out their differences, and Rock ended up buying a new house in suburban New Jersey not far from his wife so that he could easily pick up and drop off his daughters to see them. The divorce was finalized in August 2016.

Stand-up as Therapy

True to his newfound desire to mix the sad and funny threads of life, Rock was about to take as big a leap in his stand-up as he had with his directing. He had inked a deal with the video streaming service Netflix to do two original stand-up specials for the company, reportedly a $40 million deal. Netflix had gone from just streaming films to acting more like a combination of television network and movie studio.

In late 2016, Rock announced his first world tour in nine years, the Total Blackout Tour. He had not done a big tour nor put out a special since around the time

Despite a serious health scare, Rose Rock has continued to be a strong and supportive force in her son's life.

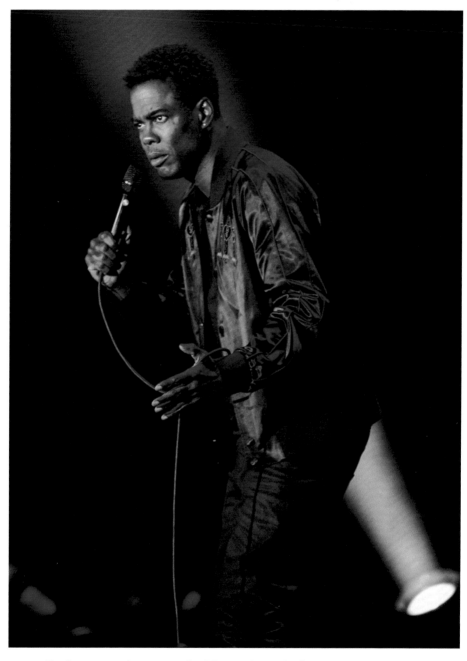

Rock paces the stage in his trademark fashion in Amsterdam in October 2017, on the European leg of his Total Blackout Tour stand-up comeback.

Barack Obama, America's first black president, had been inaugurated. It would be great fodder for his first special for Netflix, entitled *Tamborine* and recorded while on tour. For the production, Rock and his people decided to do a hometown show at the Brooklyn Academy of Music, not far from most of the places he had lived in Brooklyn over the years, and ground zero for his biggest fans.

Instead of the customary slick suit he donned for specials, he wore a T-shirt and jeans. The first half of the set featured the Rock everyone knew, openly questioning the many police shootings of unarmed blacks: "You would think the cops would occasionally shoot a white kid, just to make it look good!"[8] There was plenty of material to catch up on, including the recent surprise election of Donald Trump, racism, bullying, and more.

However, the newly divorced Rock would slow down considerably for the second half of the show, in which he shared with audiences some painful and awkward confessions about how he was at fault for the demise of his marriage. Many comedians and other performers and artists draw upon pain in their lives to make their art. For Rock, it was a way to vent about the tough couple of years he had been through. Even on this recent outing, which he joked was done mainly to pay alimony, he had suffered from the loneliness. He lamented only seeing his daughters on video chat from the isolation of hotel rooms. One day during the tour, he half-joked to *Rolling Stone*, "My own daughter has blocked me on Instagram . . . They grow up so quick."[9]

"If It Ain't New, It's Through!"

. . . .

As an artist, Chris Rock is firmly rooted in the present and future, while also looking to his lifelong influences from the past as inspiration. It is the kind of synthesis that often leads to great art. Trying to do something new and fresh has captivated him since he first set foot onstage. His motto about relationships from *Bring the Pain* can easily apply to making art, too: "If it ain't new, it's through!"[1]

On the Shoulders of Giants

Just as exciting new artists create new genres of music by combining older ones from the past, comedians like Rock study their predecessors, picking and choosing things they like and elements of a set or even simply an approach to timing and rhythm that might work for them. Some comedians playfully borrow or even steal each other's material, although too much of that can alienate fellow comedians and audiences. Rock draws inspiration from many different comedians and talents, depending on the medium he is exploring.

For example, Rock is well known for greatly admiring the work of Woody Allen. In his early years, before the internet made comedy clips easily accessible, Rock would visit the Museum of Television and Radio (now known as the Paley Center) to immerse himself in old comedy clips. Some of his favorites were Allen's films and stand-up routines. While the bombastic side of Rock's stand-up is well known, the part influenced by artists like Allen—more serious, melancholy, ironic, and self-deprecating—has always been present in Rock's work. Even his acclaimed directorial effort, *Top Five*, has been compared to Woody Allen's similarly themed 1980 comedy-drama *Stardust Memories*. In both films, the main characters play some version of their own selves. It remains to be seen what kind of films Rock helms in the next decade or so, but chances are that the comedian will lean more heavily into thoughtful scripts and character studies, as opposed to juvenile or slapstick projects.

Not all of Rock's influences are even comedians. Like his friend Eddie Murphy, Rock always admired the pop, R&B, and rock legend Prince, with whom he socialized regularly. When Prince passed away in April 2016, Rock's stage crew would put a candlelit display surrounding Prince's portrait in each dressing room on his tour. The late musician was famous for always putting out large amounts of new music. In his later concert tours, new songs always dominated in his setlists. Rock has often applied the same rule to his own tours.

Legendary musician Prince shakes hands with Rock—a longtime fan—at the 49th Annual Grammy Awards in February 2007.

A High-wire Act

Like a high-wire act walking across a tightrope dozens of feet above an audience, Rock likes to take chances. Many comedians recycle old material when going out on tour, or at least they revisit their most successful bits. Rock favors going out on a stand-up tour with all new material every time. Some fellow comedians liken this to tightrope-walking without even a safety net below to break one's fall. Jerry Seinfeld says he only adds about twenty minutes of new material to his own act each year he changes up his stand-up. He talked about Rock's approach with *Rolling Stone*: "He has an incredibly high pain tolerance because it is difficult to go out there with material that you're not sure of. To constantly go back and start over is very impressive, and a little insane."[2]

Rock also needs downtime to decompress from going out on the road. Sometimes, he waits as long as eight months or so before he gets onstage again, opting instead to write and workshop things at home. He often goes for bullet points first, figuring out what he wants to talk about, including things that have been on his mind since the last tour, before even coming up with jokes. Though Rock remains competitive, topping the last special or tour is not the most important thing. Rather, he hopes simply to remain relevant to people's experiences and to the spirit of the comedic times, too.

> **On President Donald Trump:** "We got rid of bullies, a real bully showed up, and nobody knew how to handle it."[3]

From Student to Mentor

Every new generation produces its own stand-up heroes. Rock still goes out onstage and has something to say. Nevertheless, now in his fifties, Rock belongs to a certain generation. In addition to putting milder and less frantic touches on his stand-up act, part of growing up and being a veteran comic is encouraging newer and younger talent. Many of the most popular and dynamic younger comics nowadays grew up on Rock's routines and specials. Some were inspired to do stand-up by him or benefited from his visibility and popularity, especially many African American comics. Dave Chappelle, Cedric the Entertainer, and Kevin Hart are just some of those who credit Rock's influence in their own careers and material. He has done his best to help his friends exploit his own connections, too.

One comedian and television host that Rock helped out was W. Kamau Bell. The San Francisco–based comic touches upon similar comedy terrain as Rock, including race, current events, and politics. The older comedian told Bell he thought he was funny, but that he should leave his hometown for either Los Angeles or New York to make it big. He later followed up with Bell in 2010 and helped him land his own FX network show, *Totally Biased with W. Kamau Bell*, which Rock served as executive producer on. According to Bell's interview with *The Root*, Rock advised him, "Unfamous black guys don't get TV shows. Unfamous white guys get TV shows all the time. So I want to help you get a TV show." Bell added that Rock's quiet authority impressed him: "Chris is not yelling all the time like he is in stand-up. He just very quietly has a powerful presence."[4]

Aziz Ansari is one former protégé of Rock's. The now successful stand-up comedian, actor, and filmmaker had been obsessed with Rock's seminal early works. Ansari

Comedian and *SNL* cast member Leslie Jones (*right*) joins fellow New York Knicks fan Chris Rock and a friend at a 2017 game at Madison Square Garden.

told Vulture.com, "Those two Chris Rock specials, *Bring the Pain* and *Bigger & Blacker*, in high school I knew every single word."[5] Ansari got to know Rock slowly when he ran into him at clubs and on tour, and he was blown away by the chance to interact with his hero as a peer and mentor. Rock encouraged Ansari to keep an eye out for other Indian American comics and help their careers when he could. The veteran admired Ansari's boldness (he approached Rock the first time) and respected his comedic and artistic tastes. Most of all, Rock respects comedians that work hard, and few others Rock had met could surpass Ansari's work ethic.

Yet another friend and fellow comic that Rock has helped along is Leslie Jones. The veteran road comic, friendly with Rock since both began doing stand-up in the 1980s, had felt pigeonholed and typecast as someone who could only kill it before black audiences. In 2012, she revamped her act in a big way. Rock noticed the impressive change in her material during a performance one night at the Comedy Store. Rock's connection with Lorne Michaels proved helpful. Around the time of *SNL* auditions, Michaels was looking to diversify his show's talent pool. Rock recommended Jones, insisting that she was the funniest possible pick and that Michaels should give her a chance. Jones nailed her audition and joined the cast.

Rock also had an impact on the career of close friend and collaborator Louis C.K. Since first meeting on the scene in the 1990s, Rock had established himself as a household name, but C.K.'s main work had been behind the scenes, writing for others, such as talk show

Flanked by Georgia congressman John Lewis (*left*) and California congressman Mike Thompson (*right*), Rock delivers a plea for sensible gun control legislation.

The Thirteen Greatest Stand-up Specials

On his website, Rock compiled what are, in his opinion, the thirteen best stand-up specials of all time, with short postscripts about them.

1. *Richard Pryor: Live in Concert* (1979): "The perfect concert."

2. Paul Mooney: *Know Your History: Jesus Is Black; So Was Cleopatra* (2007).

3. Dave Chappelle: *Killin' Them Softly* (2000).

4. *Eddie Murphy Delirious* (1983): "Nobody ever had a better skill set than Eddie."

5. *Bill Cosby: Himself* (1983): "The genius of this show is that not one joke is topical. Everything is timeless."

6. George Carlin: *Jammin' in New York* (1992).

7. George Lopez: *America's Mexican* (2007).

8. Steve Harvey: *One Man* (2001): "This is probably the most underrated HBO special of all time."

9. Billy Crystal: *700 Sundays* (2004).

10. Andrew "Dice" Clay: *The Day the Laughter Died* (1990).

11. Ron White: *They Call Me Tater Salad* (2004).

12. *Ellen DeGeneres: Here and Now* (2003): "Most comics just talk about what they see. This is the first time I heard somebody talk about what they feel."

13. Sam Kinison: *Louder than Hell* (1986): The last original comic whose jokes and delivery had never been done before.[6]

hosts Conan O'Brien and David Letterman. When a job as head writer and producer on Rock's old *SNL* friend Dana Carvey's show fell through after only seven episodes in 1996, C.K. remembered Rock's invitation to his HBO program. As they worked together, Rock would constantly encourage him to write his own material, for himself alone. He had so much respect for C.K., he explained to the *New York Times*, using a music analogy, "I feel like I'm James Brown, and Jimi Hendrix was in my band. He was just some kid . . . now he's back, and he's Jimi Hendrix. Is he better than me? I don't know, maybe."[7]

Staying Sharp and Relevant

The question of who is better or best on the comedy scene holds little appeal for Rock. He remembers when he was a younger comedian, Martin Lawrence opened for him and brought down the house, inspiring pangs of jealousy in him. Nowadays, he thinks less about competing with others and focuses on continuing his creative journey. There are many funny people that Rock considers great, whether he is in the mood for stand-up or cinematic comedy. Some of the comics he has named in interviews as his favorites over the years include Chris Tucker, Adam Sandler, Ellen DeGeneres, Paul Mooney, Dave Chappelle, Steve Harvey, Ron White, and many others.

The last thing Rock wants to happen to him is finding a comfort zone and being stuck within it. He sees that as a surefire way to lose all relevance and edge. Talking to *The A.V. Club*, Rock pointed out, "Comedians tend to find a comfort zone and stay there and do lamer

Giving Back

While their relationship did not last, Rock was introduced to a whole new world of philanthropy by his ex-wife. Malaak Compton-Rock and her husband have contributed their money and time to many organizations—including UNICEF, the Urban Arts Partnership, and the Elevate Hope Foundation, among many others. Rock has also performed at many star-studded charity galas to earn money for those in need. Their Angelrock Project South Africa has assisted orphans and other children, especially those stricken with AIDS and other illnesses. Back at home, the Rocks teamed up with Target to help the Salvation Army modernize dozens of libraries and other facilities, including the Salvation Army's Bushwick Community Center, which Rock himself frequented as a child. Comedian Jon Stewart has also enlisted Rock to perform at his Night of Too Many Stars, an annual event dedicated to helping fund autism research.

versions of themselves for the rest of their career. That's the average stand-up. I'm trying to be like Bob Dylan, somebody that has grown."[8]

Ultimately, critics may praise an artist's work or tear it down. Rock's philosophy is that the flesh-and-blood audience out there in front of the stand-up is the real test of someone's material and performance. He often brings up how Eddie Murphy did not win that many awards during the peak of his stand-up career, but that audience response and fandom made him among the best of all time. Asked by *The A.V. Club* what stand-up gave him that he could not find in other creative pursuits, Rock replied:

> Instant gratification. The thing about having an audience right there laughing is that critics can write what they want, but the proof is right there in front of you. I've been lucky. Critics have been overly gracious to me, but that's not that important, because the people are laughing.[9]

The Next Level

For a man who had fulfilled most of his wildest dreams by the time he turned thirty years old—*SNL*, HBO concerts, and more—it remains to be seen what direction Rock takes his career in in the coming years. He has toyed with the idea of doing more documentaries and will probably never give up stand-up, even when he takes breaks from doing routines onstage for months at a time.

Like riding a bike, it is something that comes naturally to him. He is also excited to continue expanding and growing as an artist. Fans should probably expect more

Throughout his career, Chris Rock has displayed an interest in creative growth that makes fans wonder what they can look forward to in the future.

thoughtful, Woody Allen-esque creations—like *Top Five*—as opposed to more Rock appearances in Adam Sandler films. Of course, Rock will always sign on to help a friend with a project. For instance, in 2015 he directed comedian Amy Schumer's HBO special, *Amy Schumer: Live at the Apollo*, which even earned him an Emmy nomination. Wherever his career takes him, you can be sure that Chris Rock will stay raw, real, and, above all, one of the funniest people alive.

Chronology

1965 Christopher Julius Rock III is born in Andrews, South Carolina, on February 7.

1985 Seen on screen for the first time, as an extra in *Krush Groove*.

1987 Appears in *Beverly Hills Cop II*, his first speaking film role; has a supporting guest role on *Miami Vice*.

1988 Rock's scene-stealing appearance as a thrifty fast-food patron is featured in *I'm Gonna Git You Sucka*; Christopher Julius Rock II, Rock's father, passes away after a failed surgery.

1990 Joins the cast of *Saturday Night Live* (*SNL*).

1991 Appears in a dramatic role in the black gangster epic *New Jack City*.

1992 Plays a supporting role in the Eddie Murphy vehicle *Boomerang*.

1993 Leaves *SNL*; joins the cast of *In Living Color*, which is cancelled soon after; *CB4* is released in theaters.

1994 Releases his first comedy special, *Chris Rock: Big A** Jokes*; meets future spouse, Malaak Compton.

1995 Does one of his first sitcom appearances on *The Fresh Prince of Bel-Air*.

1996 *Bring the Pain* brings Rock tremendous critical and popular acclaim; Rock covers the 1996 election for *Politically Incorrect*; returns to *SNL* to host the program; marries Malaak Compton.

1997 Premieres *The Chris Rock Show* on HBO; hosts the MTV Video Music Awards.

1998 Makes a cameo on the animated show *King of the Hill*; makes a guest appearance on *Mr. Show with Bob and David*.

1999 Releases his third stand-up special on HBO, called *Bigger & Blacker*; hosts the MTV Video Music Awards for the second time; has a supporting role in Kevin Smith's *Dogma*.

2000 Plays opposite Morgan Freeman and Reneé Zellweger in *Nurse Betty*.

2001 Appears in the widely panned but later cult classic *Pootie Tang*; stars in *Down to Earth* in one of his first bigger leading roles.

2002 Welcomes first child to the world, Lola Simone Rock, born June 28; pops up in a documentary about his friend Jerry Seinfeld, entitled *Comedian*.

2003 Directs his first film, *Head of State*, which he also stars in.

2004 Has a second child, Zahra Savannah Rock, born May 22; releases his HBO stand-up special *Never Scared*.

2005 Debuts *Everybody Hates Chris*; voices Marty the zebra in the animated smash *Madagascar*; appears in *The Longest Yard*.

2006 Directs his second film, *I Think I Love My Wife*; Does the voice of Mooseblood the mosquito in the animated film *Bee Movie*.

2008 Releases his stand-up special *Kill the Messenger.*

2009 Stars in the documentary *Good Hair,* which he conceived and developed.

2010 Stars in the well-received *Death at a Funeral* and reunites with former *SNL* costars for *Grown Ups.*

2011 Stars in his first Broadway performance, *The _____ with the Hat.*

2012 Costars in *2 Days in New York* with Julie Delpy.

2014 Writes and directs *Top Five,* considered by Rock himself and others as a creative breakthrough; begins divorce and custody proceedings with Malaak Compton-Rock.

2016 Finalizes divorce and custody issues with Compton-Rock; signs lucrative deal with Netflix for two comedy specials for $40 million; hosts the Academy Awards for the second time.

2017 Embarks on his first world tour in nine years.

2018 Debuts first Netflix special, *Tamborine,* which presents a more introspective and personal Rock talking about painful and private issues.

Chapter Notes

Chapter 1: A Rock Grows in Brooklyn

1. Danielle Brennan, "Who's the Boss? Chris Rock's Mom," Today.com, April 9, 2008, https://www. today.com/parents/who-s-boss-chris-rock-s-mom-wbna24031959.

2. "Q & A: Chris Rock," CBS News, November 30, 2014, https://www.cbsnews.com/news/q-a-chris-rock.

3. John Freeman Gill, "'Wonder Years,' by Way of Bed-Stuy," *New York Times*, December 4, 2005, http://www. nytimes.com/2005/12/04/nyregion/thecity/wonder-years-by-way-of-bedstuy.html.

4. "Chris Rock Quotes," BrainyQuote.com, Xplore Inc., 2018, https://www.brainyquote.com/quotes/chris_rock_599596.

5. Ed Pilkington, "Everybody Loves Chris," *Guardian*, January 7, 2008, https://www.theguardian.com/film/2008/jan/07/comedy.usa.

6. David A. Keeps, "Chris Rock Steps Up," *Men's Health*, May 27, 2010, https://www.menshealth.com/fitness/chris-rock-steps-up.

7. *Inside the Actors Studio*, "Chris Rock," http://www. bravotv.com/inside-the-actors-studio/season-13/videos/chris-rock (accessed February 20, 2018).

8. *Inside the Actors Studio*, "Chris Rock".

9. Kevin Chapell, "Chris Rock: Hot Comic is on the Roll of His Life," *Ebony*, May 1997, pp. 132–136.

10. David A. Keeps, "Chris Rock Steps Up," *Best Life*, April 2007, pp. 88–93.

11. Chapell, pp. 132–136.

Chapter 2: A Rising Star

1. Ed Pilkington, "Everybody Loves Chris," *Guardian*, January 7, 2008, https://www.theguardian.com/ film/2008/jan/07/comedy.usa.

2. *Rolling Stone*, "15 Things We Learned from Hanging Out with Chris Rock," May 4, 2017, https://www. rollingstone.com/culture/lists/chris-rock-15-things- we-learned-hanging-out-with-comedian-w480410.

3. Kevin Chapell, "Chris Rock: Hot Comic Is on the Roll of His Life," *Ebony*, May 1997, pp. 132–136.

4. "Q & A: Chris Rock," CBS News, November 30, 2014, https://www.cbsnews.com/news/q-a-chris-rock.

Chapter 3: Live from New York—It's Chris Rock!

1. "Chris Rock's Funniest Jokes," *Telegraph*, https://www. telegraph.co.uk/film/what-to-watch/chris-rock- oscars-funny-quotes-jokes.

2. David A. Keeps, "Chris Rock Steps Up," *Best Life*, April 2007, pp. 88–93.

3. Fred Schruers, "The Trash-Mouth Wisdom of Chris Rock," *Rolling Stone*, October 2, 1997, https:// www.rollingstone.com/culture/news/chris-rock- star-19971002.

4. Stephen Rodrick, "Chris Rock in a Hard Place: On Infidelity, His New Tour, and Starting Over," *Rolling Stone*, May 3, 2017, https://www.rollingstone.com/tv/features/chris-rock-cover-story-on-his-new-tour-and-starting-over-w479496.

5. Lee R. Schreiber, "Interview: Hey, Chris! Where'd the Edge Go?" *Los Angeles Times*, March 10, 1991, http://articles.latimes.com/1991-03-10/entertainment/ca-259_1_chris-rock.

6. "Chris Rock on the Funny Business of Finding Success," NPR, August 8, 2012, https://www.npr.org/2012/08/09/158443299/chris-rock-on-the-funny-business-of-finding-success.

7. *WTF with Marc Maron*, "Chris Rock," (podcast), November 3, 2011, http://www.wtfpod.com/podcast/episodes/episode_224_chris_rock.

8. Brian Hiatt, "Chris Rock: The Rolling Stone Interview," *Rolling Stone*, December 3, 2014, https://www.rollingstone.com/culture/features/chris-rock-the-rolling-stone-interview-20141203.

9. *WTF with Marc Maron*.

10. Brian Hiatt.

Chapter 4: Bringing the *Pain*

1. Fred Schruers, "The Trash-Mouth Wisdom of Chris Rock," *Rolling Stone*, October 2, 1997, https://www.rollingstone.com/culture/news/chris-rock-star-19971002.

2. Ibid.

3. Ethan Alter, "Emmy Flashback: Talking to the Two People Who Helped Chris Rock 'Bring the Pain,'" Yahoo! Entertainment, September 15, 2017, https://www.yahoo.com/entertainment/emmy-flashback-talking-two-people-helped-chris-rock-bring-pain-144731560.html.

4. *Chris Rock: Bring the Pain*, HBO, 1996.

5. *Never Scared*, 2004.

6. Chris Rock Quotes, BrainyQuote.com, Xplore Inc., 2018, https://www.brainyquote.com/quotes/chris_rock_450888 (accessed March 17, 2018).

7. Ray Richmond, "The Chris Rock Show," *Variety*, February 13, 1997, http://variety.com/1997/tv/reviews/the-chris-rock-show-2-1200448789.

Chapter 5: At the Top of His Game

1. Nathan Rabin, "Chris Rock," *The A.V. Club*, November 17, 2004, https://www.avclub.com/chris-rock-1798208405.

2. "Chris Rock's Funniest Jokes," *Telegraph*, https://www.telegraph.co.uk/film/what-to-watch/chris-rock-oscars-funny-quotes-jokes.

3. Roger Ebert, "*Head of State*," RogerEbert.com, March 28, 2003, https://www.rogerebert.com/reviews/head-of-state-2003.

4. Steve Weintraub, "Chris Rock Interviewed—'I Think I Love My Wife,'" Collider.com, March 13, 2007, http://collider.com/chris-rock-interviewed-i-think-i-love-my-wife.

5. A. O. Scott, "Review: 'I Think I Love My Wife': Chris Rock's Best Filmmaking Effort to Date," *New York Times*, March 15, 2007, http://www.nytimes. com/2007/03/15/arts/15iht-fmreview16.4916771. html.

6. Roger Ebert, "Good Hair," RogerEbert.com, October 7, 2009, https://www.rogerebert.com/reviews/good-hair-2009.

7. Greg Braxton, "Chris Rock Finds the Humor in 'Good Hair,'" *Los Angeles Times*, October 4, 2009, http:// articles.latimes.com/2009/oct/04/entertainment/ca-rock4.

Chapter 6: A Cut Above the Rest

1. Jon Caramanica, "Comedian, Rebranded," *New York Times*, March 3, 2011, http://www.nytimes. com/2011/03/06/theater/06rock.html.

2. Ibid.

3. Chris Rock Quotes, BrainyQuote.com, Xplore Inc., 2018. https://www.brainyquote.com/quotes/chris_rock_450875 (accessed March 17, 2018).

4. Brian Hiatt, "Chris Rock: The Rolling Stone Interview," *Rolling Stone*, December 3, 2014, https:// www.rollingstone.com/culture/features/chris-rock-the-rolling-stone-interview-20141203.

5. Jo Piazza, "Julie Delpy and Chris Rock Talk '2 Days in New York' at Sundance," *Huffington Post*, January 25, 2012, https://www.huffingtonpost. com/2012/01/25/julie-delpy-chris-rock-2-days-in-new-york_n_1231163.html.

6. Ibid.

7. Roger Ebert, "2 Days in New York," RogerEbert. com, August 15, 2012, https://www.rogerebert.com/ reviews/2-days-in-new-york-2012.

8. Brian Hiatt.

9. Ibid.

10. Lisa Kennedy, "Review: Chris Rock's 'Top Five' Nails Bawdy and Nice Notes," *Denver Post,* December 10, 2014, https://www.denverpost.com/2014/12/10/ review-chris-rocks-top-five-nails-bawdy-and-nice-notes.

11. Calvin Wilson, "'Top Five' Is Breakthrough for Chris Rock," *St. Louis Post-Dispatch*, December 11, 2014, http://www.stltoday.com/entertainment/movies/ reviews/top-five-is-breakthrough-for-chris-rock/ article_cc8c2020-4d77-5f29-9717-b412c78280aa.html.

12. Ibid.

Chapter 7: Up Close and Personal

1. Kevin Chapell, "Chris Rock: Hot Comic Is on the Roll of His Life," *Ebony*, May 1997, pp. 132–136.

2. Brian Hiatt, "Chris Rock: The Rolling Stone Interview," *Rolling Stone*, December 3, 2014, https:// www.rollingstone.com/culture/features/chris-rock-the-rolling-stone-interview-20141203.

3. "Oprah Talks to Chris Rock," *O*, June 2002, http:// www.oprah.com/omagazine/oprah-interviews-chris-rock.

4. Ibid.

5. Lauren Page, "Funnyman Chris Rock Is Serious About Parenting," WebMD, May 15, 2013, https://www.webmd.com/men/features/chris-rock-parenting#1.

6. "Q & A: Chris Rock," CBS News, November 30, 2014, https://www.cbsnews.com/news/q-a-chris-rock.

7. Terry Gross, "Chris Rock on the Funny Business of Finding Success," *Fresh Air*, August 8, 2012, https://www.npr.org/templates/transcript/transcript.php?storyId=158443299.

8. *Chris Rock: Tamborine*, Netflix, 2018.

9. Stephen Rodrick, "Chris Rock in a Hard Place: On Infidelity, His New Tour, and Starting Over," *Rolling Stone*, May 3, 2017, https://www.rollingstone.com/tv/features/chris-rock-cover-story-on-his-new-tour-and-starting-over-w479496.

Chapter 8: "If It Ain't New, It's Through!"

1. *Chris Rock: Bring the Pain*, HBO, 1996.

2. Stephen Rodrick, "Chris Rock in a Hard Place: On Infidelity, His New Tour, and Starting Over," *Rolling Stone*, May 3, 2017, https://www.rollingstone.com/tv/features/chris-rock-cover-story-on-his-new-tour-and-starting-over-w479496.

3. *Chris Rock: Tamborine*, Netflix, 2018.

4. Brett Johnson, "W. Kamau Bell: Chris Rock's TV Protege," *The Root*, August 9, 2012, https://www.theroot.com/w-kamau-bell-chris-rocks-tv-protege-1790892775.

5. Jada Yuan, "How Chris Rock Became Aziz Ansari's Mentor: 'Aziz Gets What He Wants, Man,'" Vulture.

com, May 12, 2017, http://www.vulture.com/2017/05/chris-rock-aziz-ansari-mentor.html.

6. Chris Rock, "Chris Rock's Favorite Standup Specials," ChrisRock.com, http://www.chrisrock.com/news/chris-rocks-favorite-standup-specials (accessed February 20, 2018).

7. Dave Itzkoff, "Busy Chris Rock Is Just Itching for Dirty Work," *New York Times*, August 1, 2012, http://www.nytimes.com/2012/08/05/movies/q-and-a-chris-rock-is-itching-for-dirty-work.html.

8. Nathan Rabin, "Chris Rock," *The A.V. Club*, November 17, 2004, https://www.avclub.com/chris-rock-1798208405.

9. Ibid.

Glossary

alumnus A graduate of a college, university, or other school.

blaxploitation A 1970s film genre of often low-budget cinema that centered around black characters and storylines.

bombastic Overblown or exaggerated in actions or mannerism.

cameo A brief appearance of a known actor or actress in a film or television episode.

chitlin' circuit Refers to once segregated performance venues that existed decades ago in the United States; in a modern sense, refers to clubs and music venues catering to predominantly African American audiences.

din A loud and prolonged noise.

eponymous Taking one's own name as a title.

flamboyant Showy or striking in the way one presents oneself.

gangsta rap A genre of aggressive hip-hop music that arose in the late 1980s and early 1990s depicting urban problems and realities, including crime, drugs, violence, etc.

mockumentary A fictional film shot in the style of a

documentary to satirize its subject, sometimes for humorous effect.

prolific In the arts, refers to producing large amounts of creative work.

raucous Rowdy, wild, or disorderly.

sacred idol Something that is considered impolite or unsavory to criticize or mock.

seminal Describing art works that are influential or noteworthy.

setup The first part of a joke or funny story that leads up to the payoff or punchline.

twelve-step Refers to sobriety programs that require former alcoholics or drug addicts to fulfill a checklist of twelve measures to make up for their past failings.

variety show An entertainment program or event that has a variety of different acts.

Further Reading

Books

Gitlin, Marty. *Chris Rock: A Biography of a Comic Genius.* Berkeley Heights, NJ: Enslow Publishers, 2014.

Kauffman, Susan. *Kevin Hart.* New York, NY: Enslow Publishers, 2018.

Nagle, Jeanne. *Chris Rock* (The Giants of Comedy). New York, NY: Rosen Publishing, 2015.

Todd, Anne M. *Chris Rock: Comedian and Actor.* New York, NY: Chelsea House, 2014.

Websites

NBC/Saturday Night Live Portal of Chris Rock clips
http://www.nbc.com/saturday-night-live/cast/chris-rock-14736
SNL's archive of Chris Rock–related material.

The Official Chris Rock Site
http://chrisrock.com
Chris Rock's official website.

Films

CB4, directed by Tamra Davis, Universal Pictures, 1993.

Chris Rock: Bring the Pain, directed by Keith Truesdell, HBO, 1996.

Top Five, directed by Chris Rock, Paramount Pictures, 2014.

Index

A

Academy Awards, 6, 61
All Def Comedy, 79
Allen, Woody, 15, 49, 65, 83, 97, 109
American Comedy Awards, 59
Ansari, Aziz, 100, 102
Arsenio Hall Show, The, 32–33

B

Bad Company, 63
Bee Movie, 76
Best Life, 19
Beverly Hills Cop 2, 28
Beverly Hills Ninja, 61
Big A** Jokes, 52, 53
Bigger & Blacker, 65, 102
Boomerang, 44, 77
Born Suspect, 46
Bring the Pain, 52–53, 55, 56, 65, 75, 96, 102

C

Carlin, George, 16, 24, 62, 104
Carson, Johnny, 16, 51
Carvey, Dana, 31, 105
Catch a Rising Star, 23, 24, 29
CB4, 46, 47
Cedric the Entertainer, 82, 100
Chappelle, Dave, 5, 100, 104, 105
Chris Rock Show, The, 57–59, 70
C.K., Louis, 58, 60, 63, 80, 102, 105
Comedian, 63
Comedy's Dirtiest Dozen, 29, 32
Comedy Store, 53, 102
Comic Strip Live, 24, 26
Compton-Rock, Malaak, 84, 86–87, 90, 91, 92, 106
Cosby, Bill, 15, 16, 49, 55, 104
Crouther, Lance, 63, 70
Crystal, Billy, 31, 104
Curb Your Enthusiasm, 81, 82

D

Death at a Funeral, 77
Def Comedy Jam, 51, 79
DeGeneres, Ellen, 61, 104, 105
Delpy, Julie, 79, 80
Dogma, 61–62
Down to Earth, 62–63

Dr. Doolittle, 61

E
Ebert, Roger, 42, 64, 70, 80
Emmy Awards, 55, 57, 59, 109
Everybody Hates Chris,
    67–69

F
Farley, Chris, 35, 38, 44, 61
Fresh Prince of Bel-Air, The, 52

G
Garofalo, Janeane, 62
George, Nelson, 47, 52
Good Hair, 70–71
Gregory, Dick, 15, 49
Grown Ups, 77

H
Hall, Arsenio, 28, 32, 33,
    40, 51
Hart, Kevin, 82, 100
Hartman, Phil, 31, 47, 61
HBO Comedy Half-Hour, 52
Head of State, 63–65, 69
Homicide: Life on the Street,
    52

I
Ice Cube, 41, 47
Ice-T, 42, 70

I'm Gonna Git You Sucka,
    28–29
In Living Color, 29, 41,
    44–45, 46
I Think I Love My Wife,
    69–70

J
Jones, Leslie, 82, 102

K
Kill the Messenger, 72
Krush Groove, 27

L
Lawrence, Martin, 51, 52,
    77, 105
LeRoi, Ali, 63, 67
Long, Nia, 70, 71
Louie, 80, 81

M
Madagascar, 76
*Madagascar: Escape 2
    Africa*, 76
Maron, Marc, 41, 44
Martin, 52
Martin, Steve, 15, 49, 55, 61
Meadows, Tim, 39, 77
Michaels, Lorne, 30, 32, 35,
    37, 39, 42, 44, 102
Morgan, Tracy, 31, 77, 82
Moxy Show, The, 52

Murphy, Eddie, 23, 24, 26–28, 31, 33, 37, 40, 44, 55, 61, 97, 107

N
NAACP Image Awards, 59, 68
Never Scared, 65
New Jack City, 42, 44, 47, 73
Night Flight, 29
Nurse Betty, 62, 77
N.W.A., 41, 47

O
Obama, Barack, 80, 95
O'Brien, Conan, 31, 105
Osmosis Jones, 63

P
Politically Incorrect with Bill Maher, 55, 64
Pootie Tang, 63
Pryor, Richard, 15, 16, 24, 49, 55, 61, 104

R
Rocca, Mo, 12, 30, 88
Rock, Chris
   early life, 8–20
   as mentor, 99–105
   personal life, 70, 79, 84–95
Roll with the New, 57
Rudolph, Maya, 31, 77

S
Sandler, Adam, 35, 38, 44, 76, 77, 82, 105, 109
Saturday Night Live, 5, 6, 23, 30–32, 34–44, 46, 47, 59, 61, 74, 75, 77, 80, 102, 105, 107
Schneider, Rob, 35, 38, 77
Seinfeld, Jerry, 63, 76, 82, 99
Sgt. Bilko, 61
Spade, David, 35, 38, 77
Stewart, Jon, 61, 106
Sykes, Wanda, 58, 60

T
Tamborine, 95
Tonight Show, The, 16, 51
Top Five, 80–83, 97
Total Blackout Tour, 92, 95
2 Days in New York, 77, 79–80

U
Uptown Comedy Express, 28

W
Washington, Kerry, 69, 70
Wayans, Damon, 33, 51
Wayans, Keenen Ivory, 28–29, 41, 45
Williams, Tyler James, 67
Winfrey, Oprah, 86, 87, 88